the vineyard cookbook

the vineyard cookbook

seasonal recipes & wine pairings inspired by America's vineyards

by barbara scott-goodman

Food Photography by Colin Cooke

With Landscape Photography by Kirk Irwin and Wes Walker

welcome
BOOKS

new york • san francisco

autumn menus

winter menus

wineries

Artesa Vineyards & Winery, Napa Valley, California

Barboursville Vineyards, Barboursville, Virginia

Beaulieu Vineyard, Napa Valley, California

Bedell Cellars, Long Island, New York

Benton-Lane Winery, Willamette Valley, Oregon

Channing Daughters Winery, Bridgehampton, New York

Chateau St. Jean Winery, Sonoma Valley, California

Chateau Ste. Michelle Winery, Columbia Valley, Washington

Clos Du Val Winery, Napa Valley, California

Cooper Mountain Vineyards, Cooper Mountain, Oregon

Cuvaison Estate Wines, Napa Valley, California

Dolce Winery, Napa Valley, California

Duckhorn Vineyards, Napa Valley, California

Far Niente Winery, Napa Valley, California

Fox Run Vineyards, Finger Lakes, New York

Gloria Ferrer Winery, Sonoma Valley, California

Goldeneye Winery, Anderson Valley, California

Hedges Family Estate, Red Mountain, Washington

Lafond Winery & Vineyard, Santa Rita Hills, California

Merryvale Vineyards, Napa Valley, California

Mumm Napa, Napa Valley, California

Nickel & Nickel Vineyards, Napa Valley, California

Paraduxx, Napa Valley, California

Peju Province Winery, Napa Valley, California

Rancho Sisquoc Winery, Santa Maria Valley, California

Sanford Winery & Vineyards, Santa Rita Hills, California

Seven Hills Winery, Columbia Valley, Washington

Sterling Vineyards, Napa Valley, California

Talley Vineyards, Arroyo Grande Valley, California

V. Sattui Winery, Napa Valley, California

Willamette Valley Vineyards, Willamette Valley, Oregon

Zaca Mesa Winery & Vineyards, Santa Ynez Valley, California

introduction

Welcome to *The Vineyard Cookbook,* a delicious compendium of menus, recipes, and wine pairings from outstanding wineries and vineyards from all over the country.

When I consider cooking, I like to take full advantage of ingredients in season, at the time of year when they are most flavorful. Springtime means fresh oysters, asparagus, and strawberries. Summer afternoons and nights call for casual picnics and barbecues that use the best and freshest seafood and produce of the season. I savor the earthy flavors of autumn and enjoy cooking intimate dinners that feature them. And on cold winter days and nights I love to serve casual comfort-food dishes, like lamb stew and bread pudding, as well as festive party food for the holidays. Here is a collection of many of my favorite seasonal recipes that I have enjoyed cooking for family and friends who have gathered at my table over the years. These are uncomplicated, ingredient-driven meals that are a pleasure to prepare, serve, and eat, no matter what the season.

And what to drink with these meals? The opening of a bottle of wine immediately transforms any meal into something special, but I, like many people, find the art of pairing food and wine often mystifying. Our featured wineries have taken the guesswork and confusion out of this process, providing wine-savvy suggestions that will equip you with the knowledge you need. Whether you desire a good inexpensive table wine to share with friends for an informal meal or a great vintage for a special evening, you may feel confident in selecting appropriate wines that pair well with the variety of dishes in this book, from appetizers to desserts. Wine experts from a wide range of vineyards will be your guides, with thoughtful, interesting, and wonderful wine suggestions in three price ranges.

Read on and sip, savor, taste, and enjoy!

WINE PRICES

●
$15.00 to $25.00

● ●
$25.00 to $35.00

● ● ●
$35.00 and over

spring menus

Toast the first days of spring with rich and fruity Chardonnay, Sauvignon Blanc, or Fumé Blanc and enjoy a sumptuous dinner of creamy oyster soup, fresh salmon, and first-of-the-season asparagus, strawberries, and rhubarb.

oyster, scallion & watercress soup

Fresh, briny oysters add just the right touch to this elegant, creamy soup. Whether you shuck the oysters yourself or have your fishmonger do it, be sure that the oyster liquor is reserved. And when cooking them, be sure not to overcook. Remove the soup from the heat as soon as the edges of the oysters begin to curl—no later.

18 SMALL OYSTERS IN SHELLS, WELL SCRUBBED

2 TABLESPOONS UNSALTED BUTTER

5 TO 6 SCALLIONS, TRIMMED AND MINCED

4 MEDIUM CARROTS, PEELED AND CUT INTO JULIENNE ABOUT 1½ INCHES LONG

2 CUPS DRY WHITE WINE

2 CUPS HALF-AND-HALF

½ CUP HEAVY CREAM

2 CUPS STEMMED WATERCRESS (1 TO 2 BUNCHES)

KOSHER SALT AND FRESHLY GROUND BLACK PEPPER

LEMON SLICES, FOR GARNISH

continued

continued

welcome spring dinner

OYSTER, SCALLION & WATERCRESS SOUP

—

SALMON STEAKS IN ORANGE-LIME MARINADE

—

CHILLED ASPARAGUS VINAIGRETTE

—

ORZO WITH FRESH LEMON & HERBS

—

STRAWBERRY RHUBARB SUNDAES

1. Shuck the oysters over a bowl and reserve the liquor. Strain the liquor through 1 or 2 thicknesses of dampened cheesecloth into another bowl. Set both the oysters and the liquor aside.

2. Melt the butter in a skillet over medium-high heat. Add the scallions and sauté for about 3 minutes until just softened. Set aside.

3. Cook the carrots in boiling salted water to cover for about 2 minutes, until just tender. Drain immediately and rinse under cold water to stop the cooking. Pat them dry and set aside.

4. In a large nonreactive saucepan or stock pot, bring the wine to a boil. Remove the pan from the heat. Slowly stir in the half-and-half and heavy cream. Stir the mixture constantly to prevent curdling. When well mixed, return the pan to the heat and bring to a slow boil. Cook uncovered over high heat for about 5 minutes, until slightly thickened.

5. Reduce the heat to medium-low and stir in the reserved oyster liquor. Add the scallions and carrots and cook for about 5 minutes, until heated through. Season to taste with salt and pepper.

6. Add the watercress and cook gently for about 5 minutes longer, until heated through. Add the oysters and stir briskly for about 1 minute, until their edges just begin to curl. Immediately ladle the soup into bowls and garnish by floating lemon slices on top.

SERVES 6

WINE PAIRING

●
Chateau St. Jean Sonoma County Fumé Blanc 2007

Fox Run Vineyards Arctic Fox

Sterling Vintner's Collection Sauvignon Blanc 2007

Willamette Valley Vineyards Pinot Gris 2007

●●
Cuvaison Napa Valley Carneros Chardonnay 2006

Zaca Mesa Z Gris 2007

●●●
Far Niente Napa Valley Estate Bottled Chardonnay 2006

fox run *finger lakes, new york*

NOTABLE FOR BEING the only North American winery to win a gold medal in France's Riesling du Monde competition in 2007, Fox Run Vineyards is renowned for producing world-class dry whites. Fox Run was named one of the top wineries of 2008 by *Wine & Spirits* magazine.

Their enchanting Rieslings, offering aromas as diverse as lime peel, wet minerals, and tropical fruits, are especially exciting, and the winery is much lauded for its Pinot Noir, Cabernet Franc, and Lemberger.

Located in the heart of New York's Finger Lakes region, the property offers a stunning vista of Seneca Lake along with sweeping vineyards and a not-to-be-missed spacious tasting room.

sterling   *napa valley, california*

STERLING VINEYARDS is among the most visited and most reviewed destination wineries in the Napa Valley. Founded in 1964, Sterling Vineyards sits atop a 400-foot knoll accessible by aerial tram, and offers stunning views of the surrounding wine country. The winery achieved international recognition when its wine won first place in the Ottawa Wine Tasting of 1981.

Sterling is known for its popular Napa Valley Cabernet Sauvignon and produces quality varietal wines, including Sauvignon Blanc, Chardonnay, Merlot, and Pinot Noir.

salmon steaks
in orange-lime marinade

This tempting dish is quick to prepare and cooks in a matter of minutes on the grill or under the broiler.

1 TEASPOON WHITE WINE VINEGAR

JUICE OF 3 ORANGES

JUICE OF 3 LIMES

6 CLOVES GARLIC, THINLY SLICED

1 TEASPOON OLIVE OIL

1/3 CUP FINELY CHOPPED CILANTRO

KOSHER SALT AND FRESHLY GROUND BLACK PEPPER

6 1-INCH-THICK SALMON STEAKS (ABOUT 2¼ POUNDS)

CHOPPED FRESH CILANTRO, FOR GARNISH

WINE PAIRING

•
Chateau Ste. Michelle Columbia
  Valley Sauvignon Blanc 2007

Fox Run Vineyards Reserve Chardonnay

••
Channing Daughters Mudd Vineyard
  Sauvignon Blanc

Clos Du Val Chardonnay 2006

Cuvaison Napa Valley Carneros
  Pinot Noir 2006

V. Sattui Napa Valley Sauvignon
  Blanc 2007

•••
Lafond Vineyard Lafond Chardonnay

Nickel & Nickel Medina Vineyard
  Chardonnay 2006

Sterling Reserve Chardonnay 2005

1. In a shallow glass or ceramic bowl, whisk together the vinegar, orange and lime juice, and garlic. Add the olive oil, whisking until blended. Stir in the 1/3 cup cilantro and season to taste with salt and pepper. Lay the salmon steaks in the bowl and carefully turn to coat with the marinade. Cover and let the salmon marinate for 30 to 60 minutes at room temperature, turning the fish once.

2. Prepare a charcoal or gas grill or preheat the broiler.

3. Transfer the salmon and the marinade to a shallow roasting pan. Grill or broil the salmon steaks for 5 to 6 minutes to a side, until flaky but still moist.

4. Serve each steak with a tablespoon of the cooked marinade drizzled over the top and garnish with cilantro.

SERVES 6

chilled asparagus vinaigrette

Fresh asparagus is one of the first sure signs of spring, and one of the best ways to serve it is chilled with a simple vinaigrette.

2 1/2 POUNDS FRESH ASPARAGUS, TRIMMED AND PEELED, IF NECESSARY

2 CLOVES GARLIC, FINELY MINCED

PINCH OF KOSHER SALT

1 TABLESPOON DIJON MUSTARD

1 TABLESPOON RED WINE VINEGAR

1 TABLESPOON FRESH LEMON JUICE

1/2 CUP EXTRA-VIRGIN OLIVE OIL

FRESHLY GROUND BLACK PEPPER

1/4 CUP CHOPPED FRESH FLAT-LEAF PARSLEY, FOR GARNISH

1. In a large skillet, bring salted water to a boil, add the asparagus spears and bring back to a boil. Reduce the heat and simmer for about 4 to 6 minutes, until the asparagus is just tender. Drain and rinse under cold water, then pat dry with paper towels. Arrange the asparagus in a shallow serving dish.

2. In a small bowl, mix together the garlic, salt, mustard, and vinegar to make a paste. Whisk in the lemon juice and oil until well blended. Season to taste with pepper. Pour the vinaigrette over the asparagus.

3. Chill the asparagus thoroughly. Garnish with parsley before serving.

SERVES 6

orzo with fresh lemon & herbs

Orzo, tiny rice-shaped pasta, is a wonderful side dish that is compatible with salmon as well as grilled chicken and lamb.

8 OUNCES ORZO (ABOUT 1⅓ CUPS)

1 TABLESPOON UNSALTED BUTTER, AT ROOM TEMPERATURE

½ CUP CHOPPED FRESH HERBS,
   SUCH AS FLAT-LEAF PARSLEY, CILANTRO, CHIVES, AND BASIL

1 TABLESPOON FRESH LEMON JUICE

KOSHER SALT AND FRESHLY GROUND BLACK PEPPER

1. Bring a medium pot of salted water to a boil over high heat. Add the orzo and cook according to package directions. Drain immediately and transfer to a medium bowl. Stir in the butter and mix well.

2. Stir in the herbs and lemon juice and season to taste with salt and pepper. Serve immediately.

SERVES 6

strawberry rhubarb sundaes

This recipe for strawberry rhubarb sauce is a springtime treat. It's good with many flavors of ice cream or yogurt, over pound cake, or as a topping for fresh berries. It freezes well, too, for as long as a month.

2 CUPS FRESH RHUBARB (2 TO 3 LARGE STALKS), FINELY DICED

1 PINT FRESH STRAWBERRIES, HULLED AND HALVED

1/3 CUP WATER

1/3 CUP CRÈME DE CASSIS

1/3 CUP SUGAR

6 SCOOPS VANILLA ICE CREAM OR FROZEN VANILLA YOGURT

6 LARGE STRAWBERRIES WITH STEMS, FOR GARNISH

1. Put the rhubarb, strawberries, water, crème de cassis, and sugar in a large nonreactive saucepan. Bring to a boil over high heat, stirring. Lower the heat and simmer, uncovered, for 20 to 30 minutes until the mixture thickens, stirring occasionally.

2. Let the sauce cool to room temperature, or refrigerate it for later use. The sauce may be refrigerated for 2 to 3 days or frozen for up to 1 month.

3. Put a scoop of ice cream or yogurt in a large dessert bowl. Spoon the sauce over the ice cream and top with a large strawberry. Repeat to make 6 sundaes.

SERVES 6

WINE PAIRING

•
Benton-Lane Pinot Noir Rosé

••
Gloria Ferrer Blanc de Noirs
Rancho Sisquoc Late Harvest
  Sauvignon Blanc 2005

•••
Bedell Blanc de Blancs 2004
Mumm Napa DVX 2000

Gather friends and family around the table and celebrate the pleasures of spring—longer days, blooming flowers, and fresh fruit and vegetables—with this wonderful Italian-inspired dinner.

crostini

Crostini are perfect to serve at intimate get-togethers as well as big cocktail parties. These delicious nibbles, which pair very well with both red and white wine, always say welcome. Crostini (Italian for "little toasts") are sliced rounds from a baguette that are brushed with olive oil and lightly toasted or baked. Crostini are a snap to toast in the oven. Arrange baguette slices on a baking sheet and bake until lightly browned and crisp. They are delicious with many kinds of toppings—prosciutto and cheese, chicken liver mousse, tapenade, crabmeat salad, hummus, or soft cheese spread, to name just a few.

12 (1/2-INCH-THICK) SLICES FROM A BAGUETTE
3 LARGE CLOVES GARLIC, HALVED
OLIVE OIL, FOR BRUSHING
TOPPING OF CHOICE (RECIPES FOLLOW)

Preheat the oven to 400°F. Arrange the bread slices in a single layer on a baking sheet and bake until golden brown and crispy, about 5 minutes. Rub garlic on one side of each slice and brush lightly with olive oil. Top the crostini with desired toppings and serve.

MAKES 12 CROSTINI OR 6 SERVINGS

springtime pasta dinner

WARM GREENS & CHICKPEA CROSTINI
RICOTTA & PROSCIUTTO CROSTINI

—

LINGUINE WITH FRESH ASPARAGUS & PEAS

—

GOLDEN WALNUT CAKE WITH FRESH BERRIES & CINNAMON CREAM

warm greens & chickpea crostini

2 TABLESPOONS OLIVE OIL

3 CUPS MIXED FRESH GREENS, SUCH AS BABY SPINACH, SWISS CHARD,
   OR WATERCRESS, RINSED, STEMMED, AND COARSELY CHOPPED

1 (15.5-OUNCE) CAN CHICKPEAS, RINSED AND DRAINED

2 TABLESPOONS DRY WHITE WINE

PINCH RED PEPPER FLAKES

KOSHER SALT AND FRESHLY GROUND BLACK PEPPER

WINE PAIRING

•

Rancho Sisquoc Riesling 2006

••

Cuvaison Napa Valley Carneros
Chardonnay 2006

Lafond Vineyard Santa Rita Hills
Chardonnay

V. Sattui Family Chardonnay 2006

1. Heat 1 tablespoon olive oil in a large skillet or sauté pan over medium heat. Add the greens and sauté until wilted, about 3 minutes. Transfer to a bowl.

2. In the same pan, heat the remaining 1 tablespoon olive oil. Add the chickpeas, wine, red pepper flakes, and salt and pepper to taste. Sauté until the wine is reduced and the chickpeas are heated through, about 5 minutes.

3. Top each crostini with warm greens and then chickpeas, and serve.

MAKES 12 CROSTINI OR 6 SERVINGS

SAUVIGNON BLANC

French for "wild white," this particular grape grows as vigorously as its name suggests. Along with their unbridled growth, Sauvignon Blanc grapes tend to have a musky flavor to them that can be fresh and crisp. In general, wines made from this grape are tart and tangy. When chilled, they can be an excellent complement to a number of cheeses as well as fresh fish.

California is the leading producer of Sauvignon Blanc (sometimes called Fumé Blanc) in North America. Washington State also provides North America with some excellent Sauvignon Blancs. In general, these grapes do not have to ferment for long and are best enjoyed at a young vintage.

ricotta & prosciutto crostini

12 VERY THIN SLICES PROSCIUTTO

ABOUT ½ CUP RICOTTA CHEESE, AT ROOM TEMPERATURE

FRESHLY GROUND BLACK PEPPER

Top each crostini with a slice of prosciutto and a spoonful of the cheese.
Add freshly ground black pepper and serve.

MAKES 12 CROSTINI OR 6 SERVINGS

WINE PAIRING

•

Fox Run Vineyards Riesling

Rancho Sisquoc Sauvignon Blanc 2007

••

Duckhorn Vineyards Napa Valley
   Sauvignon Blanc

Sanford Santa Barbara County
   Chardonnay 2006

Zaca Mesa Grenache 2006

•••

Dolce 2005

Lafond Vineyard Santa Rita Hills
   Pinot Noir

sanford *santa rita hills, california*

SANTA BARBARA WINE COUNTRY got a jump-start from Sanford. Back in 1971, Sanford Winery discovered an overlooked grape-growing treasure in the Santa Rita Hills. Recognizing a magical combination of climate and soil conditions much like those in France's famed Burgundy province, Sanford planted the area's first Pinot Noir in its now iconic Sanford and Benedict Vineyard, frequently named a top vineyard of California. Farmed sustainably under Terlato family ownership, today, Sanford turns out a Chardonnay and Pinot Noir that rank among the best and most distinctive in the world. Sanford's leadership helped put Santa Barbara and the Santa Rita Hills on the map of the world's great wine regions.

Winemaker and General Manager Steve Fennell has a simple philosophy when it comes to grape growing and winemaking: treat the soil with respect, grow consistent and high-quality grapes, and craft elegant, fruit-forward wines that are the finest expression of the Santa Rita Hills. Along with its acclaimed wines, Sanford's landmark adobe winery and tasting room have received their share of accolades. The winery was recognized in 2006 by *Wine & Spirits* magazine as one of the top examples of winery architectural design in the United States.

linguine with fresh asparagus & peas

This is a simple and wonderful dish to serve for a casual, elegant dinner party.

1 POUND FRESH ASPARAGUS, TRIMMED AND RINSED

1 CUP SHELLED FRESH PEAS

2 TABLESPOONS OLIVE OIL

1 TABLESPOON GARLIC, FINELY CHOPPED

1/2 CUP CHOPPED SHALLOTS

1 CUP HEAVY CREAM

1 POUND LINGUINE

1/2 CUP FRESHLY GRATED PARMESAN CHEESE, PLUS MORE FOR SERVING

SALT AND FRESHLY GROUND BLACK PEPPER

ZEST OF 1/2 LEMON, FINELY MINCED

1. Bring a saucepan of salted water to a boil, add the asparagus and boil until just tender, 3 to 6 minutes. Drain and set aside. When cool enough to handle, cut the spears into 2-inch pieces.

2. Bring a saucepan of salted water to a boil, add the peas and boil until just tender, 2 to 4 minutes. Drain and rinse immediately under cold water. Drain well and set aside.

3. In a skillet large enough to hold all of the cooked pasta, sauté the garlic and shallots over medium heat until softened. Add the cream and cook over low heat until thickened, about 5 minutes. Remove from the heat and set aside.

WINE PAIRING

•
Rancho Sisquoc Sylvaner 2007

••
Channing Daughters Tocai Friulano
Chateau St. Jean Robert Young
  Chardonnay 2005
Mumm Napa Brut Prestige
Talley Bishop's Peak
  Santa Barbara County Pinot Gris

•••
Nickel & Nickel Searby Vineyard
  Chardonnay 2006

4. Meanwhile, cook the linguine in a large pot of salted boiling water until just tender. Drain but do not rinse.

5. Add the asparagus and peas to the sauce and bring to a low simmer over medium heat. Add the linguine and toss to coat well. Add the Parmesan, salt and pepper to taste, and the lemon zest, and toss well. Serve immediately with additional grated cheese.

SERVES 6

golden walnut cake
with fresh berries & cinnamon cream

An easy cake to make, this is lovely topped with a mix of fresh berries and sweetened, cinnamon-spiced whipped cream.

cake:

1¼ CUPS UNBLEACHED ALL-PURPOSE FLOUR

1 TEASPOON BAKING POWDER

PINCH OF SALT

½ CUP (1 STICK) UNSALTED BUTTER, AT ROOM TEMPERATURE, CUT INTO PIECES

1 CUP SUGAR

2 LARGE EGGS, AT ROOM TEMPERATURE, SEPARATED

½ CUP MILK

1 CUP CHOPPED WALNUTS

1 TEASPOON PURE VANILLA EXTRACT

2 CUPS MIXED FRESH BERRIES,
   SUCH AS STRAWBERRIES, RASPBERRIES, BLUEBERRIES AND BLACKBERRIES

½ CUP SUGAR

topping:

1 CUP HEAVY CREAM

1 TABLESPOON SUGAR

1 TEASPOON GROUND CINNAMON

1. Preheat the oven to 350°F. Lightly butter and flour a 9-inch round cake pan and tap out the excess flour.

2. To prepare the cake, in a bowl, combine the flour, baking powder, and salt, and whisk 8 to 10 times, until well mixed.

3. Using an electric mixer set on medium-high speed, cream the butter and sugar. Add the egg yolks and beat until smooth. Add the dry ingredients in 3 or 4 batches, alternating with the milk and ending with the dry ingredients. Stir well, and then fold in the nuts and vanilla.

4. Beat the egg whites on medium-high speed, until they hold stiff peaks. Fold the whites into the batter just until mixed. Spread the batter in the cake pan. Bake on the center oven rack for 35 to 40 minutes or until a toothpick inserted in the center comes out clean. Turn out onto a wire rack to cool.

5. Combine the berries in a large bowl. Sprinkle with sugar and toss. Set aside at room temperature for about 20 minutes to give the juices time to accumulate and sweeten.

6. To make the topping, set the electric mixer on medium-high and whip the cream and sugar until the cream is thick but not dry. Add the cinnamon and continue whipping until the cream is the desired consistency. Serve the cake topped with the berries and cream.

SERVES 6 TO 8

WINE PAIRING

•
Beaulieu Vineyards Muscat de Beaulieu
Rancho Sisquoc Sylvaner 2007
••
Barboursville Phileo
Zaca Mesa Late Harvest Viognier 2007
•••
Artesa Codorniu Napa Grand Reserve

RIESLING

Riesling grapes produce highly acidic white wines that tend to be sweet and reminiscent of citrus fruits. This combination of sugar and acid is the reason for Riesling wines' versatility when paired with food. Working deliciously with pork and white fish, they also serve well with spicier cuisines, such as Indian and Thai. Rieslings also pair very nicely with not-too-sweet desserts and fruit. California, New York's Finger Lakes region, Oregon, and Washington have soil that is perfect for the growth of Riesling grapes.

artesa *napa valley, california*

ARTESA IS ONE of the most architecturally stunning wineries in North America.
Sitting on 350 acres, this ultra-modern winery offers panoramic views of Napa Valley, the
Carneros growing region, and San Francisco Bay. Steeped in the property's modernistic,
minimalist look and surrounded by contemporary sculptures, fountains, and reflecting pools,
the Visitor Center and Tasting Room are a delight to behold.

Artesa Vineyards and Winery has constructed an ideal environment in which to create
wines of uncompromising quality. It opened in 1991 and began as a producer of sparkling
wines, but the winery has since found its niche in still wines, especially their Estate Pinot Noir
and Napa Valley Cabernet Sauvignon.

Winemaker Dave Dobson, who joined Artesa in 2005, says, "Our Napa Cabernet has
intense dark-berry fruit flavor with a plush, rich volume that coats and lingers, and the
Estate Pinot Noir, which is grown in the hillsides surrounding the winery, has an old-world
elegance with bold new-world fruit and power."

No matter what the occasion, spring is all about new beginnings. What better way to savor the season than to serve exquisite food and fine wine for friends and catch up after a long winter?

lemon-fennel olives

This preparation is a great way to enhance any type of olive. The olives, which can be prepared up to a month ahead of time, are layered with fennel and lemon slices, and then they marinate in fruity olive oil.

1½ POUNDS OLIVES, DRAINED AND RINSED

1 LEMON, THINLY SLICED

½ BULB FENNEL, TRIMMED AND THINLY SLICED LENGTHWISE

4 CLOVES GARLIC, THINLY SLICED

1 TABLESPOON BLACK PEPPERCORNS

1 TABLESPOON FENNEL SEEDS

EXTRA-VIRGIN OLIVE OIL, TO COVER

1. Put a layer of olives in the bottom of a 1-pint glass jar. Add several slices of the lemon, fennel, and garlic, and sprinkle with some of the peppercorns and fennel seeds. Continue layering until the jar is full. Cover the olives with olive oil and seal the jar tightly. Repeat this process with a second 1-pint jar.

2. Refrigerate the olives for 24 hours before serving. They may be stored in the refrigerator for up to 1 month. Bring to room temperature before serving.

MAKES TWO 1-PINT JARS

festive spring meal

LEMON-FENNEL OLIVES

SPICY ROASTED PARTY NUTS

SMOKED SALMON SALAD
WITH DILL VINAIGRETTE

PORK LOIN
WITH ORANGE-MARMALADE
GLAZE

ROASTED SWEET POTATOES
& RED ONIONS

GINGER-ORANGE SNAP PEAS

RICOTTA CHEESECAKE

peju province   *napa valley, california*

A FAMILY-OWNED BUSINESS, Peju Province was founded in 1982 by Anthony and Herta Peju, who together with daughters Lisa and Ariana, strive to make stunning wines. This requires a combination of winemaking skills and blending; but above all, the Peju approach seeks to capture the essence of the grapes from the *terroir* in which they are grown.

Their well-known Estate Reserve Cabernet Sauvignon, made from grapes harvested from their organic Rutherford H. B. Vineyard (the initials of Herta's maiden name, Herta Behensky) is the perfect mix of the H. B. Vineyard's deep, gravelly soil, early morning fog, and lengthy, sunny days. Another favorite is the Napa Valley Zinfandel, a supple 100 percent Zinfandel from the Persephone Vineyard that displays flavors of strawberry and raspberry jam, chocolate, and anise.

spicy roasted party nuts

Nuts baked with pan-toasted spices are always a welcome treat. They can be made up to a week ahead of time and are an excellent snack to serve before dinner or when friends drop in for a glass of wine.

1/2 TEASPOON GROUND CUMIN

1/2 TEASPOON CHILI POWDER

1/2 TEASPOON GARLIC SALT

1/2 TEASPOON GROUND GINGER

1/2 TEASPOON GROUND CINNAMON

PINCH OF CAYENNE PEPPER

1 TABLESPOON OLIVE OIL

2 CUPS MIXED NUTS, SUCH AS PECANS, ALMONDS, CASHEWS, OR WALNUTS

KOSHER SALT

1. Preheat the oven to 325°F.

2. In a small bowl, mix the spices together. Heat the oil in a small skillet over medium heat. Add the spice mixture and cook to blend, stirring constantly, about 3 minutes.

3. Put the nuts in a large mixing bowl, add the spice mixture and toss well to coat. Spread the nuts on a baking sheet and bake until toasted, about 12 minutes, shaking the pan occasionally. Remove the nuts from the oven, sprinkle with salt to taste and let cool for at least one hour. The nuts can be made up to a week ahead of time and stored in airtight containers.

MAKES 2 CUPS

WINE PAIRING

•

Barboursville Pinot Grigio 2007

••

Artesa Tempranillo 2005

Gloria Ferrer Blanc de Blancs 2004

Lafond Vineyard Santa Rita Hills Pinot Noir

Peju Carnival 2007

•••

Duckhorn Vineyards Napa Valley Merlot

Far Niente Napa Valley Estate Bottled Chardonnay 2006

smoked salmon salad with dill vinaigrette

Smoked salmon is always elegant to serve as starter. Here it is chopped into a tartare with red onions and capers, served over greens, and topped with a tasty vinaigrette laced with fresh dill.

½ POUND SMOKED SALMON, CUT INTO SMALL PIECES

3 TABLESPOONS FINELY CHOPPED RED ONION

1½ TABLESPOONS CAPERS, DRAINED

2 TABLESPOONS FRESH LEMON JUICE

1½ TABLESPOONS OLIVE OIL

FRESHLY GROUND BLACK PEPPER TO TASTE

vinaigrette:

2 TABLESPOONS DIJON MUSTARD

1 TABLESPOON WHITE WINE VINEGAR

3 TABLESPOONS EXTRA-VIRGIN OLIVE OIL

2 TEASPOONS WHOLE MILK

PINCH OF SUGAR

2 TABLESPOONS CHOPPED FRESH DILL

4 CUPS MIXED SALAD GREENS

DILL SPRIGS, FOR GARNISH

WINE PAIRING

●

Barboursville Vintage Rosé 2007

● ●

Beaulieu Vineyards Napa Valley Chardonnay 2005

Bedell Cellars Taste White 2007

Channing Daughters Brick Kiln Chardonnay

Cooper Mountain Vineyards Pinot Noir

Gloria Ferrer Sonoma Brut

● ● ●

Artesa Estate Pinot Noir 2006

Lafond Vineyard Arita Hills Pinot Noir

Talley Vineyards Rincon Vineyard Pinot Noir

Willamette Valley Vineyards Estate Vineyard Pinot Noir 2006

1. Put the salmon, onion, capers, lemon juice, olive oil, and pepper in a bowl and mix together gently.

2. To make the vinaigrette, whisk the mustard and vinegar together. Add the olive oil and whisk again. Slowly add the milk, sugar, and dill, and whisk again. Taste and adjust the seasonings.

3. Arrange the greens on six salad plates. Spoon the salmon tartare over the greens, drizzle each serving with vinaigrette, garnish with dill sprigs, and serve at once.

SERVES 6

channing daughters *bridgehampton, new york*

SOME SAY CHANNING DAUGHTERS has a wine wizard, winemaker James Christopher Tracy. Though the vineyard is a producer of excellent whites, rosés, and outstanding reds, he is also an experimenter who plays with both expected and exotic grape varieties to craft a wide array of small-production whites. The *New York Times* raves that every vintage brings new expectations from Channing Daughters. In fact, the only problem is that there often isn't enough of it to go around.

The popular Mudd Vineyard Sauvignon Blanc is a clean, refreshingly fruity yet herbaceous white that never fails to impress. And the *Times* also says, "The Meditazione is designed to woo the intellect as well as the digestive system." Full of apricot, citrus, caramel, and spice, it sells out almost as fast as it's made.

pork loin
with orange-marmalade glaze

Succulent and flavorful—few meats surpass pork loin. It's low in fat, cooks in less then two hours, and blends well with any number of basting sauces and glazes. This sweet glaze, made with pan drippings and orange marmalade, is especially good.

1 BONELESS CENTER-CUT PORK LOIN (3½ TO 4 POUNDS)

1 TABLESPOON OLIVE OIL

KOSHER SALT AND FRESHLY GROUND BLACK PEPPER

2 TEASPOONS FRESH ROSEMARY LEAVES OR 1 TEASPOON DRIED ROSEMARY

1 CUP DRY WHITE WINE

1 CUP WATER

½ CUP ORANGE MARMALADE

1. Preheat the oven to 350°F.

2. Put the pork loin on a rack in a shallow roasting pan. Brush the meat with olive oil and then sprinkle it with salt, pepper, and rosemary. Pour the wine and water into the roasting pan. Roast for 1 hour.

3. Remove the pan from the oven and spoon ½ cup of pan drippings into a small bowl. Add the marmalade and mix well. Pour this mixture over the meat and return it to the oven.

4. Continue roasting the meat for 35 to 45 minutes, basting it 2 to 3 times with pan drippings, until a meat thermometer reaches 160°F.

5. Let the meat rest for 15 minutes before serving. Skim any fat from the pan drippings and serve with the roast.

SERVES 6

WINE PAIRING

•
Fox Run Vineyards Cabernet
   Franc Lemberger

••
Cuvaison Napa Valley Carneros
   Pinot Noir 2006
Sterling Napa Valley Merlot 2005
Willamette Valley Vineyards
   Willamette Valley Pinot Noir 2006

•••
Channing Daughters Meditazione
Goldeneye Anderson Valley
   Pinot Noir

roasted sweet potatoes & red onions

Sweet potatoes are not just for serving during the winter holidays. In the springtime, they are a lovely counterpoint to boldly flavored pork roast and snap peas.

6 YAMS, PEELED AND CUT INTO $1/2$-INCH DICE

4 RED ONIONS, PEELED AND QUARTERED

2 OR 3 TABLESPOONS OLIVE OIL

KOSHER SALT AND FRESHLY GROUND BLACK PEPPER

1. Preheat the oven to 350°F.
2. Arrange the sweet potatoes and onions in an aluminum-foil-lined roasting pan and sprinkle with the olive oil, shaking the pan to coat them evenly. Season to taste with salt and pepper. Roast for 1 to $1^{1}/_{2}$ hours, stirring occasionally, until very tender. Serve immediately.

SERVES 6

MERLOT

Merlot grapes continue to produce wine for the wine devotee. While Merlots have flavor similar to Cabernet Sauvignons, they are less acidic and thus leave a fuller flavor on the palate. The smaller levels of acidity in Merlots make them drinkable at a young vintage. California, Long Island, the Niagara Peninsula, and Virginia are among the top producers of Merlots in the United States.

Herbal and spicy pepper, bay leaf, and clove, as well as smoky oak, dominate a glass of Merlot, accentuating the deep flavors of black cherry, currant, and plum, and make it well-suited for savory dishes. Most Merlots pair well with meats such as pork, veal, lamb, and sausage. Those serving pasta dishes or pizza should also consider a Merlot with their meal.

ginger-orange snap peas

Quickly cooked sugar snap peas with an added dash of fresh ginger and orange zest are a delightful springtime side dish. Snow peas may be substituted in this recipe.

1 POUND FRESH SUGAR SNAP PEAS, TRIMMED

1 TEASPOON RICE VINEGAR

2 TABLESPOONS EXTRA-VIRGIN OLIVE OIL

2 TEASPOONS GRATED ORANGE ZEST

1 TABLESPOON FINELY GRATED GINGER

KOSHER SALT AND FRESHLY GROUND BLACK PEPPER

1. Bring a large pot of salted water to a boil. Add the snap peas and cook until crisp-tender, about 2 minutes. Drain and transfer to a large bowl.

2. In a small bowl, whisk together the vinegar, olive oil, orange zest, and ginger. Pour over the snap peas and toss to combine. Season to taste with salt and pepper. Serve warm, cold, or at room temperature.

SERVES 6

ricotta cheesecake

The light taste and texture of cheesecake made with ricotta cheese instead of the more common cream cheese is amazing.

4 CUPS RICOTTA CHEESE

1½ CUPS GRAHAM CRACKER CRUMBS (FROM ABOUT 20 SQUARES)

6 TABLESPOONS (¾ STICK) UNSALTED BUTTER, MELTED

¾ CUP SUGAR

4 LARGE EGGS

1 CUP HEAVY CREAM

⅓ CUP FINELY CHOPPED ALMONDS

1 TEASPOON ALMOND EXTRACT

WINE PAIRING

•

Chateau St. Jean Riesling 2007

Rancho Sisquoc Riesling 2006

••

Cooper Mountain Vineyards Pinot Blanc 'Vin Glace'

Mumm Napa Cuvée M

•••

Chateau St. Jean Late Harvest Riesling 2005

Gloria Ferrer Carneros Cuvée 1998

1. Place the ricotta in a sieve over a bowl and let drain 1 hour.

2. Preheat the oven to 350°F. Lightly butter a 9-inch springform pan. In a mixing bowl, combine the crumbs, melted butter, and ¼ cup sugar. Blend well. Transfer to the prepared springform pan and press with the back of a wooden spoon or your fingertips to evenly cover the bottom and partway up the sides of the pan. Bake the crust 10 minutes. Cool completely on a wire rack.

3. Reduce the heat to 325°F.

4. In a large mixing bowl with an electric mixer on low speed, beat the drained ricotta and remaining ½ cup sugar. Beat in the eggs, one at a time, until smooth. Add the cream, almonds, and almond extract and beat until smooth. Pour into the prepared crust. Bake until the center is firm, 1 hour. Cool to room temperature in the pan on a rack, then refrigerate until chilled, at least 2 hours (or up to 24 hours).

5. Remove the cheesecake from the pan by releasing the sides; transfer to a plate.

SERVES 6 TO 8

gloria ferrer   *sonoma valley, california*

GLORIA FERRER CAVES & VINEYARDS, in the heart of Sonoma's picturesque Carneros region, is where seven generations of European winemaking tradition skillfully combines with state-of-the-art winemaking techniques. The winery is dedicated to the production of wines that reflect the artistry of the winemaker and the "marriage of vine to place" in the vineyard. Fruit is cultivated for premium-quality sparkling and still wines on 335 acres of estate vineyards distinguished by warm days, cool nights, summer fog, and a long growing season that coaxes grapes to maturity slowly and consistently, with balanced sugar and acidity. Gloria Ferrer's still wines complement the sparkling wines that will always remain the first love of the Ferrer family.

The winery is a vibrant blend of Catalan and California mission design. Its expansive tasting room, or the sun-drenched Vista Terrace that overlooks the winery's estate vineyards, provides the perfect place to enjoy a glass of sparkling or still wine with savory Spanish and local cheeses, meats, almonds, and other delicacies.

summer menus

Left: Zaca Mesa Winery & Vineyard, Santa Ynez Valley, California

Summer entertaining should be simple and casual. This al fresco barbecue makes the most of delicious seasonal fare and couldn't be easier to prepare.

cherry tomato & sweet corn salsa

Take advantage of summer's glorious bounty with this tasty salsa that is made of red and yellow cherry tomatoes, a red bell pepper, and sweet corn.

3 MEDIUM EARS CORN

2 CUPS CHERRY TOMATOES, PREFERABLY A MIX
   OF RED AND YELLOW, STEMMED, AND HALVED

1 MEDIUM RED BELL PEPPER, SEEDED, DEVEINED, AND DICED

1 MEDIUM RED ONION, CUT INTO 1/4-INCH DICE

6 SCALLIONS, TRIMMED AND MINCED

1/2 CUP CHOPPED FRESH CILANTRO

2 TABLESPOONS BALSAMIC VINEGAR

2 TABLESPOONS FRESH LIME JUICE

2 TEASPOONS GROUND CUMIN

KOSHER SALT AND FRESHLY GROUND BLACK PEPPER

1. Bring a large pot of water to a boil. Add the corn, return to a boil, and cook for 5 minutes. Drain the corn. When cool enough to handle, scrape the kernels off the cob.

2. Transfer the corn to a large bowl. Add the tomatoes, pepper, onion, scallions, cilantro, vinegar, lime juice, cumin, and salt and pepper to taste. Toss gently to mix. Set aside at for 1 hour. Serve at room temperature or chilled. The salsa will keep for up to a week in the refrigerator.

MAKES 3 CUPS

summer barbecue

CHERRY TOMATO &
SWEET CORN SALSA

GUACAMOLE

GRILLED SIRLOIN STEAK
WITH PORT MARINADE

ROASTED POTATO SALAD
WITH ARUGULA
& GOAT CHEESE

GREEN & YELLOW
STRING BEANS

BLUEBERRY & PEACH CAKE

guacamole

No summer barbecue is complete without a bowlful of gorgeous green guacamole. There are many ways to make it and this simple, straightforward version is one of the best.

3 RIPE AVOCADOS, HALVED, PITTED, AND COARSELY CHOPPED

2 TABLESPOONS FRESH LIME JUICE

1/2 RED ONION, DICED

1/2 RIPE TOMATO, COARSELY CHOPPED

PINCH OF GROUND CUMIN

KOSHER SALT

DASH OF HOT SAUCE

1. Scoop the avocado into a medium bowl. Add the lime juice and mash lightly with a fork.

2. Gently mix in the onion, tomato, and cumin, and continue to mash. Season to taste with the salt and hot sauce and mash again until well mixed but not too smooth. Serve at once.

MAKES ABOUT 2 1/2 CUPS

WINE PAIRING

●
Rancho Sisquoc Sylvaner 2007

● ●
Channing Daughters Tre Rosati
Peju Carnival 2007
Seven Hills Columbia Valley
Tempranillo 2005

● ● ●
Artesa Napa Valley Cabernet
Sauvignon 2005
V. Sattui Eagle Point Vineyard
Zinfandel 2006

goldeneye *anderson valley, california*

GOLDENEYE BEGAN MAKING premium-quality, cool-climate Pinot Noir from its estate winery in the Anderson Valley in 1997. Blending grapes from four estate vineyards planted to nineteen clones of Pinot Noir on eleven different rootstocks, Goldeneye is dedicated to crafting wines of refinement and elegance from a rich palette of *terroir*-inspired fruit. Reflecting the Mendocino Coast's unique marine influences, sites, and soils, these grapes create an elegant, sophisticated Pinot.

To further enhance natural depth and complexity, winemaker Zach Rasmuson selects only a small percentage of the finest fruit for each vintage before applying small-lot, artisan winemaking techniques.

grilled sirloin steak
with port marinade

Summer just wouldn't be summer without grilled steak. Marinating the beef in full-bodied port mixed with a bit of lemon juice and fresh rosemary tenderizes the beef while adding rich flavor. It is best to marinate the steak for at least two hours.

2 TABLESPOONS OLIVE OIL

JUICE OF 1/2 LEMON

1 TEASPOON SUGAR

1 TABLESPOON CHOPPED FRESH ROSEMARY
  OR 1 TEASPOON DRIED ROSEMARY

4 CLOVES GARLIC, THINLY SLICED

1 CUP PORT

FRESHLY GROUND BLACK PEPPER

3 POUNDS 1-INCH-THICK SIRLOIN

WINE PAIRING

•
Sterling Vintner's Collection
  Zinfandel 2005

••
Fox Run Vineyards Meritage
Gloria Ferrer Carneros Merlot 2005
Hedges Family Estate Three
  Vineyards 2006
Sanford Santa Rita Hills
  Santa Barbara County Pinot Noir 2006
Talley Bishop's Peak Edna Valley Syrah

•••
Bedell Cellars Bedell Musée 2006
Benton-Lane First Class Pinot Noir
Duckhorn Vineyards Napa Valley
  Cabernet Sauvignon
Goldeneye Anderson Valley Pinot Noir
Merryvale Napa Valley Merlot 2005
Peju Napa Valley Cabernet
  Sauvignon 2005
Zaca Mesa Black Bear Syrah 2005

1. To make the marinade, combine the olive oil, lemon juice, sugar, rosemary, garlic, port, and pepper to taste in a small bowl.

2. Put the steak in a glass or ceramic dish and pour the marinade over it. Cover and refrigerate for at least 2 hours and up to 8 hours. Turn the steak occasionally.

3. Prepare a gas or charcoal grill. Grill the steak over medium-hot coals for 4 to 5 minutes to a side for rare and 6 to 7 minutes for medium. Baste several times during grilling with the marinade.

4. Remove the steak to a platter and slice on the diagonal into 3/8-inch slices. Pour any accumulated juices over the meat and serve.

SERVES 6

hedges family estate *red mountain, washington*

THE HEDGES FAMILY ESTATE has focused on the concept of *terroir*—the natural relationship between topography, soil, and microclimate—since 1987. Located in the premier growing region of Red Mountain in Washington State, the winery produces excellent Cabernet Sauvignon, Merlot, and Hedges Family Estate Three Vineyards, their flagship wine. As the name implies, the wine is a blend from their three vineyards, Red Mountain Vineyard, Hedges, and the youngest, Bel'Villa.

Going a step beyond organic farming, Hedges began a three-year biodynamic certification process in January 2007. They believe this commitment to *terroir,* combined with respect for our natural resources, produces wines that are pure and distinctive. Hedges Family Estate Three Vineyards wines are characterized by dark, concentrated aromas and flavors of blackberry and plum with hints of licorice. The fruit is integrated with toast, cinnamon, clove, and cola on a core of firm tannins and balanced acidity. This wine will drink well now, but will also continue to age beautifully over the next 5 to 10 years.

roasted potato salad with arugula & goat cheese

There are a few tricks to making this smashing roasted potato salad—be sure to roast the potatoes very slowly and to add the vinaigrette to the potatoes while they are still warm.

3 POUNDS SMALL RED NEW POTATOES (ABOUT 12 POTATOES), HALVED OR QUARTERED

8 UNPEELED CLOVES GARLIC

KOSHER SALT

1/3 CUP OLIVE OIL

vinaigrette:

2 TEASPOONS GRAINY MUSTARD

1 TABLESPOON BALSAMIC VINEGAR

1/2 CUP EXTRA-VIRGIN OLIVE OIL

3/4 TO 1 CUP STEMMED ARUGULA

4 OUNCES FRESH GOAT CHEESE, CRUMBLED

FRESHLY GROUND BLACK PEPPER

2 TEASPOONS EXTRA-VIRGIN OLIVE OIL

1. Preheat the oven to 300°F.

2. In a roasting pan, toss the potatoes with the garlic cloves, salt to taste, and add olive oil. Bake for 1 1/2 to 2 hours, until the potatoes are fork-tender. Lower the heat to 250°F if the potatoes are cooking too quickly.

3. To make the vinaigrette, whisk the mustard and vinegar together in a small bowl. Slowly add the olive oil, whisking constantly until the vinaigrette thickens.

4. To make the salad, take the potatoes from the oven and scrape them into a large bowl. Pour the vinaigrette over the warm potatoes and gently toss them with the dressing. Add the arugula and toss again.

5. Heap the potato salad into a large shallow bowl or platter. Sprinkle the crumbled cheese over the top. Season to taste with pepper and drizzle with olive oil. Serve the salad warm or at room temperature.

SERVES 6

green & yellow string beans

This is a lovely way to serve fresh beans, particularly since they can be made ahead of time and served chilled or made shortly before eating and served at room temperature. Use the freshest green and yellow beans you can find for this dish.

¾ POUND GREEN BEANS, ENDS TRIMMED

¾ POUND YELLOW BEANS, ENDS TRIMMED

1 TABLESPOON FRESH LEMON JUICE

⅓ CUP EXTRA-VIRGIN OLIVE OIL

1 TABLESPOON BALSAMIC VINEGAR

KOSHER SALT AND FRESHLY GROUND BLACK PEPPER

¼ CUP CHOPPED FRESH FLAT-LEAF PARSLEY, FOR GARNISH

1. Cook the green and yellow beans in enough lightly salted boiling water to cover for about 2 minutes, until crisp-tender. Drain and rinse under cold running water. Drain again.

2. Put the beans in a large ceramic or glass bowl, sprinkle with the lemon juice and toss.

3. In a small bowl, whisk together the olive oil and vinegar and .season to taste with salt and pepper.

4. Pour over the beans and toss well. Chill the beans or serve at room temperature. Garnish with fresh parsley just before serving.

SERVES 6

blueberry & peach cake

This cake takes advantage of fresh blueberries and midsummer peaches when they are at their peak.

BUTTER AND FLOUR, FOR BAKING PAN

1 CUP UNBLEACHED ALL-PURPOSE FLOUR

1 TEASPOON BAKING POWDER

^{1}/$_2$ CUP (1 STICK) UNSALTED BUTTER, SOFTENED

^{1}/$_2$ CUP FIRMLY PACKED LIGHT BROWN SUGAR

^{1}/$_2$ CUP PLUS 3 TABLESPOONS GRANULATED SUGAR

2 LARGE EGGS, AT ROOM TEMPERATURE

2^1/$_2$ CUPS RIPE PEACHES (ABOUT 3 PEACHES), PEELED AND THINLY SLICED

1 CUP FRESH BLUEBERRIES

^{1}/$_2$ TEASPOON GROUND CINNAMON

WINE PAIRING

•

Chateau St. Jean Sonoma County
   Riesling 2007

••

Cuvaison Napa Valley Carneros
   Chardonnay 2006

Mumm Napa Cuvée M

•••

Nickel & Nickel John's Creek
   Vineyard Chardonnay 2006

1. Preheat the oven to 350°F. Lightly butter and flour an 8-inch square baking pan.

2. In a medium bowl, whisk together the flour and baking powder.

3. In a large bowl, using an electric mixer on high speed, cream the butter, brown sugar, and ^{1}/$_2$ cup of the granulated sugar for about 3 minutes, until light and fluffy. With the mixer running on medium speed, add the flour mixture to the batter a little at a time; do not overmix. Beat in the eggs.

4. Scrape the batter into the prepared pan. Smooth the surface and then arrange the sliced peaches and blueberries on top of the batter.

5. In a small bowl, combine the remaining 3 tablespoons sugar with the cinnamon and sprinkle the mixture over the peaches.

6. Bake for about 1 hour, or until the cake begins to pull away from the sides of the pan and turns golden brown. Remove the cake from the oven and cool in the pan on a wire rack. When completely cool, serve the cake directly from the pan or remove it from the pan, cut it into squares, and serve it fruit-side up.

SERVES 6 TO 8

mumm napa *napa valley, california*

MUMM NAPA IS ONE of America's top producers of sparkling wine and one of the most popular destinations for Wine Country visitors. For more than 20 years, Mumm Napa sparkling wines have set the standard for California *méthod traditionnelle,* emphasizing the qualities of Napa Valley fruit along with the unique, casual elegance of Napa Valley Style. *Wine Enthusiast* magazine calls Mumm Napa "one of America's Best Tasting Rooms."

The region's proximity to the Pacific Ocean and San Pablo Bay brings cool evening temperatures, fog, wind, and low rainfall. The effect produces Chardonnay with naturally crisp acidity and great depth of flavor. It also allows the Pinot Noir fruit grown in this region to develop rich flavors of fresh raspberry, berry, bright cherry, and spice.

Lazy summer afternoons were made for picnics. Eating, sipping wine, and relaxing with friends at the beach, on the porch, or under a shady tree is what the season is all about.

sunny afternoon picnic

CREAMY CARROT
& CHIVE SOUP

❧

BUTTERMILK BISCUITS

❧

CHICKEN, WATERCRESS
& WALNUT SALAD

❧

HEIRLOOM TOMATO,
BASIL & FETA CHEESE SALAD

❧

MINTED FRUIT
SUGAR COOKIES OR BISCOTTI

creamy carrot & chive soup

Fill up a thermos full of chilled creamy carrot soup with fresh chives. Served with buttermilk biscuits, it's a perfect picnic starter.

2 TABLESPOONS UNSALTED BUTTER

3 MEDIUM WHITE ONIONS, CHOPPED

3 CUPS CHICKEN BROTH, PREFERABLY HOMEMADE

6 LARGE CARROTS, PEELED AND DICED

2 LARGE RUSSET POTATOES, PEELED AND DICED

PINCH OF CAYENNE PEPPER

KOSHER SALT AND FRESHLY GROUND BLACK PEPPER

1. Melt the butter in a large soup pot over medium heat and sauté the onions for about 5 minutes, until softened.

2. Add the broth, 2 cups of water, carrots, and potatoes. Bring to a boil, reduce the heat, and simmer, partially covered, for about 25 minutes until the vegetables are very tender. Remove the pot from the heat and let the soup cool.

3. Purée the soup in batches in a blender or food processor until very smooth. Return the soup to the pot. Season to taste with the cayenne, salt, and pepper.

4. Chill the soup in the refrigerator for at least 4 hours. Serve the soup cold, garnished with fresh chives.

SERVES 6

WINE PAIRING

•

Beaulieu Vineyard Coastal Estates
  Riesling 2006

• •

Benton-Lane Pinot Blanc
V. Sattui Gamay Rouge 2007

buttermilk biscuits

These biscuits are a wonderful accompaniment to soup and salad. They're also terrific to serve spread with sweet butter and paper-thin slices of prosciutto or honey-baked ham as an hors d'oeuvre.

2 CUPS UNBLEACHED ALL-PURPOSE FLOUR

1 TABLESPOON SUGAR

1 TABLESPOON BAKING POWDER

1 TEASPOON SALT

1/2 TEASPOON BAKING SODA

1/4 CUP VEGETABLE SHORTENING, CHILLED

2 TABLESPOONS UNSALTED BUTTER, CHILLED

2/3 CUP BUTTERMILK

1. Preheat the oven to 450°F.

2. Put the flour, sugar, baking powder, salt, and baking soda into the bowl of a food processor and pulse briefly to mix. Add the shortening and butter, and pulse 6 to 8 times, until the mixture resembles coarse meal. Transfer to a bowl and blend in enough of the buttermilk to form a soft dough.

3. On a lightly floured work surface, knead the dough a few times until the dough holds together. Roll or pat the dough to a thickness of 1/4 to 1/2 inch. Using 2- to 2 1/2-inch round biscuit or cookie cutters or an upturned glass, cut biscuits and transfer to an ungreased baking sheet. Gather the scraps of dough, pat out again and cut more biscuits. Bake for 10 to 15 minutes, until golden brown.

MAKES ABOUT 12 BISCUITS

chicken, watercress & walnut salad

This excellent version of chicken salad is great for picnics because it tastes best at room temperature.

½ CUP DRY WHITE WINE

1 ONION

2 CARROTS

2 RIBS CELERY, TRIMMED AND HALVED

12 SPRIGS FRESH FLAT-LEAF PARSLEY

12 BLACK PEPPERCORNS

KOSHER SALT

3 WHOLE CHICKEN BREASTS (ABOUT 3 POUNDS), SPLIT

½ CUP WALNUT HALVES, TOASTED (SEE NOTE ON PAGE 000)

vinaigrette:

1 TABLESPOON DIJON MUSTARD

1 TABLESPOON WHITE WINE VINEGAR

1 TEASPOON SUGAR

⅓ CUP EXTRA-VIRGIN OLIVE OIL

KOSHER SALT AND FRESHLY GROUND BLACK PEPPER

1 BUNCH WATERCRESS, STEMMED

1 TO 2 TABLESPOONS WALNUT OIL, FOR DRIZZLING

WINE PAIRING

•
Chateau St. Jean Sonoma County Chardonnay 2007

Fox Run Vineyards Chardonnay

Sterling Napa County Sauvignon Blanc 2007

••
Benton-Lane Pinot Gris 2007

Clos Du Val Ariadne 2006

Gloria Ferrer Carneros Chardonnay 2006

Peju Persephone Vineyard Chardonnay 2007

•••
Far Niente Estate Bottled Chardonnay Napa Valley 2006

1. Put the wine, onion, carrots, celery, and parsley in a large soup pot. Add about 4 quarts water, the peppercorns, and 1 tablespoon salt. Bring to a boil, reduce the heat, and simmer, uncovered, for 15 minutes.
2. Add the chicken breasts to the simmering broth, raise the heat, and return to a boil. Reduce the heat and gently simmer, partially covered, until the chicken is cooked through, about 25 to 30 minutes. Remove the pot from the heat and let the chicken cool in the broth. *continued*

3. Remove the chicken from the broth. Strain the broth and reserve for another use. Tear the chicken into bite-sized pieces, discarding the skin and bones, and put in a large bowl. Add the walnuts.

4. In a small bowl, whisk together the mustard, vinegar, and sugar. Slowly add the olive oil, whisking constantly, until the vinaigrette thickens. Pour over the chicken and walnuts and gently toss together until well mixed. Season to taste with salt and pepper.

5. Arrange the watercress on a large platter and spoon the chicken salad over it. Drizzle with walnut oil and serve at room temperature.

SERVES 6

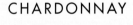

CHARDONNAY

While the Cabernet Sauvignon holds the title as the king of red wine grapes, the Chardonnay grape is the king of white wines. This grape produces wine that is full-bodied and rich in flavor. A sip of Chardonnay should fill the palate with hints of fruity flavors such as pear, melon, fig, apple, lemon, and pineapple. At the same time, spicy and nutty flavors accent the overall flavor of the Chardonnay without overpowering its fruitiness.

Chardonnays tend to pair well with white-meat dishes like chicken and turkey as well as light seafood. Those that have a stronger oak flavor, however, do not pair as well with such dishes, but complement smoked fish and foods with garlic. The buttery flavors in Chardonnay make it less suitable for acidic foods such as tomato dishes.

clos du val *napa valley, california*

CLOS DU VAL WAS FOUNDED in 1972 in what would later be known as the Stags Leap District of the Napa Valley. The winery's first vintage was one of six California Cabernet Sauvignons chosen for the legendary Paris Tasting, where California wines outscored the French.

Clos Du Val's classically styled wines were created by Bordeaux-born founder and wine-maker Bernard Portet and his partner, John Clews. Together, the two built the winery's reputation for Cabernet Sauvignon, which makes up the majority of the winery's production. Typical Clos Du Val Cabernet characteristics include cassis and blackberry flavors, with hints of olive, leather, and toasty oak. These wines are full-bodied yet balanced, making them an ideal accompaniment for food.

Clos Du Val also makes Chardonnay, Pinot Noir, and Merlot, as well as a limited amount of Ariadne, a proprietary blend of Semillon and Sauvignon Blanc named after the wife of Dionysus, the Greek god of wine. This winery's ivy-covered building and well-manicured rose garden set the scene for a romantic wine-tasting experience.

heirloom tomato, basil & feta cheese salad

Heirloom tomatoes are definitely worth seeking out at your local farmers' market. Their unique shapes and vibrant colors—yellow, orange, white, and shades of green and purple—are beautiful in salads, like this very simple one made with feta cheese. When making this salad, use the finest-quality ingredients you can find.

6 ASSORTED RIPE HEIRLOOM TOMATOES (ABOUT 3 POUNDS),
   CORED AND CUT INTO LARGE WEDGES
1/2 RED ONION, THINLY SLICED
1/2 CUP THINLY SLICED BASIL LEAVES
1 TABLESPOON BALSAMIC VINEGAR
3 TABLESPOONS EXTRA-VIRGIN OLIVE OIL
FRESHLY GROUND BLACK PEPPER
3/4 CUP (ABOUT 1/2 POUND) CRUMBLED FETA CHEESE
1 TABLESPOON DRAINED CAPERS

1. Put the tomatoes, onion, and basil in a large bowl and toss gently to combine.

2. In a small bowl, whisk together the vinegar and oil until well blended. Pour over the tomato mixture and gently toss to combine. Season to taste with pepper.

3. Top the salad with the crumbled cheese and sprinkle with the capers. Serve at room temperature.

SERVES 6

talley   *arroyo grande valley, california*

THE TALLEY FAMILY'S INTEREST in farming started in 1948, when Oliver and Hazel Talley first began growing vegetables in the Arroyo Grande Valley. In 1982, that interest spread to their son, Don Talley, who planted a test plot of different grape varieties including Pinot Noir and Chardonnay in what is now the West Rincon Vineyard. Four years later, Talley Vineyards produced its first wine in a small winery adjacent to one of the Talley Farms vegetable coolers. In the fall of 1991, a state-of-the-art winery was completed at the foot of the Rincon Vineyard, where Talley Vineyards estate wines and Bishop's Peak wines are handcrafted. A tasting room with sweeping vistas of the vineyards and vegetable fields was completed in 2003 and third-generation family member Brian Talley now serves as president of Talley Vineyards and Talley Farms.

Winemaker Leslie Mead and Vineyard Manager Kevin Wilkinson focus on the reflection of *terroir* in the finished product, using classical Burgundian methods. They strive for the highest quality in Talley Vineyards wines, aiming for consistency from vintage to vintage.

minted fruit

There is nothing better to eat on a picnic than a bowl of chilled, perfectly ripe summer fruit—peaches, plums, and melon—served with a hint of fresh mint. Biscotti or sugar cookies are an excellent accompaniment.

3 RIPE PEACHES, PEELED, PITTED, AND SLICED

6 SMALL RIPE PLUMS, PITTED AND SLICED

1/2 RIPE MELON, SUCH AS HONEYDEW, CANTALOUPE, OR CRENSHAW, SEEDED AND CUT INTO 1/2-INCH CUBES OR BALLS (ABOUT 2 CUPS)

1/4 CUP CHOPPED FRESH MINT

Place the peaches, plums, melon, and mint in a large bowl and toss together. (Note that the flavor of mint intensifies over time. If you prefer a less minty flavor, add the mint to the salad about an hour before serving.) Refrigerate for about 2 hours.

SERVES 6

WINE PAIRING

●
Beaulieu Vineyard Coastal Estates
    Riesling 2006
Chateau Ste. Michelle
    Columbia Valley Riesling 2006
● ●
Channing Daughters Vino Bianco
Hedges Family Estate Three
    Vineyards 2006
Talley Bishop's Peak Pinot Gris 2007
● ● ●
Dolce 2005

Enjoy a lovely, leisurely dinner filled with summer's bounty that begins with an extravagant lobster dish, and ends with a cobbler filled with delicious ripe peaches and raspberries.

lobster, corn & tomato salad

This truly indulgent salad made with fresh lobster, corn, and tomatoes is a peak-of-summer treat.

6 CUPS COOKED LOBSTER MEAT (SEE NOTE)

4 CUPS COOKED CORN KERNELS (FROM 4 EARS FRESH CORN)

3 RIPE TOMATOES, COARSELY CHOPPED

3 RIBS CELERY, DICED

1/2 CUP CHOPPED FRESH FLAT-LEAF PARSLEY

3 TABLESPOONS CHOPPED FRESH CHIVES

vinaigrette:

2 TABLESPOONS WHITE WINE VINEGAR

5 TABLESPOONS EXTRA-VIRGIN OLIVE OIL

PINCH OF CAYENNE PEPPER

KOSHER SALT AND FRESHLY GROUND BLACK PEPPER

4 CUPS MIXED SALAD GREENS

*elegant
summer dinner*

LOBSTER, CORN & TOMATO
SALAD

GRILLED TUNA
WITH MANGO SALSA

GRILLED
SUMMER VEGETABLES

BLACK-BEAN SALAD

PEACH & RASPBERRY
COBBLER

1. Put the lobster, corn, tomatoes, celery, parsley, and chives in a large bowl and gently toss together.

2. In a small bowl, whisk together the vinegar, olive oil, cayenne pepper, and salt and pepper to taste. Pour the vinaigrette over the lobster mixture and toss gently to combine. Taste and adjust the seasonings, if necessary. Cover and chill the salad for up to but no longer than 2 hours before serving.

3. Arrange the salad greens on a large platter. Spoon the salad over the greens and serve at once.

SERVES 6

Note: A 1- to 1¼-pound lobster will yield about 1 cup of cooked lobster meat. When buying lobster for making salad or lobster rolls, look for culls (one-clawed lobsters); they are usually less expensive.

WINE PAIRING

•
Seven Hills Columbia Valley Riesling 2007

• •
Chateau St. Jean La Petite Étoile Fumé Blanc 2006

Gloria Ferrer Royal Cuvée 2001

Sterling Napa Valley Chardonnay 2006

Talley Vineyards Oliver Vineyard Chardonnay

• • •
Far Niente Napa Valley Oakville Estate Bottled Cabernet Sauvignon 2005

Lafond Vineyard Lafond Chardonnay

ZINFANDEL

Zinfandel is the most commonly planted grape in California. Wines from this grape have a slightly sweet flavor to them. In general, these wines tend to bring out the flavors of cranberry, boysenberry, raspberry, blackberry, and black cherry. This fruitiness makes the wine perfect for stewed meats or savory dishes containing fruit.

paraduxx   *napa valley, california*

COMPLETED IN FALL 2005, the Paraduxx winery is located in the center of the Napa Valley along the less-traveled Silverado Trail. The architectural centerpiece of the estate is its unique ten-sided fermentation building that houses the contemporary winemaking facility.

Its signature wine, Paraduxx, is a boldly elegant Napa Valley red wine. Fusing the robust flavors of California's native Zinfandel with the grandeur of Cabernet Sauvignon, Paraduxx embraces the best of both core varietals. An unabashed extrovert, this innovative blend has the personality to mix naturally with great food and dynamic company. Free from convention, Paraduxx has developed its own exuberant personality filled with enticing layers of lush fruit and engaging aromatics.

v. sattui   *napa valley, california*

FOUNDED IN 1885 in San Francisco by Vittorio Sattui, an Italian immigrant, V. Sattui was reestablished in St. Helena in 1975 by great-grandson Dario Sattui. V. Sattui wines are sold only at the winery, not in stores or restaurants anywhere. Its more than 300 acres of vineyards produce 40,000 cases of wine.

More than 40 award-winning wines are offered to accommodate every taste and budget. V. Sattui specializes in single-vineyard Cabernets and Zinfandels, but is also known for its excellent Rieslings, a Gamay Rouge, and a solera-made Madeira. Another favorite is the Sattui Family White—a Chardonnay, Semillon, Sauvignon Blanc, off-dry Riesling, and Muscat blend—which has an aftertaste of Asian pear.

grilled tuna with mango salsa

Salsas are not only for serving with chips, they are also terrific with grilled seafood, chicken, and meat. Try this tasty one made with a mango and plum tomatoes as a lively accompaniment to grilled tuna.

2 PLUM TOMATOES, SEEDED AND CHOPPED INTO ¼-INCH PIECES

1 LARGE RIPE MANGO, PEELED AND DICED

½ MEDIUM RED ONION, FINELY CHOPPED

½ MEDIUM RED PEPPER, SEEDED, DEVEINED,
    AND CUT INTO ¼-INCH PIECES

1 CLOVE GARLIC, FINELY MINCED

PINCH OF RED PEPPER FLAKES

2 TABLESPOONS CHOPPED FRESH CILANTRO LEAVES

1 TABLESPOON ORANGE JUICE

1 TABLESPOON WHITE VINEGAR

2 TABLESPOONS FRESH LIME JUICE

KOSHER SALT AND FRESHLY GROUND BLACK PEPPER

6 1-INCH-THICK TUNA STEAKS (ABOUT 2½ POUNDS)

OLIVE OIL, FOR BRUSHING

WINE PAIRING

•
Rancho Sisquoc Sauvignon Blanc 2007

••
Artesa Estate Chardonnay 2006
Cuvaison Napa Valley Carneros
    Syrah 2005
Fox Run Vineyards Pinot Noir
Sanford Santa Barbara County
    Chardonnay 2006
Seven Hills Viognier 2007

•••
V. Sattui Henry Ranch Pinot Noir 2006

1. Combine the tomatoes, mango, onion, pepper, garlic, pepper flakes, and cilantro in a large nonreactive bowl and mix gently. Whisk the orange juice, vinegar, and lime juice together. Add to the tomato mixture and mix gently. Season to taste with salt and pepper. Chill in the refrigerator for at least one hour before serving. The salsa will keep in the refrigerator for up to 3 days.

2. Prepare a gas or charcoal grill. Brush the tuna steaks lightly with olive oil. Grill the tuna for about 5 minutes on each side until flaky but still moist.

3. Spoon some salsa into the center of each plate. Place a tuna steak on top of it and spoon more salsa over the fish. Serve immediately.

SERVES 6

grilled summer vegetables

When grilling vegetables, be sure to marinate them or brush them with olive oil before cooking to eliminate the raw taste that quick-grilling sometimes leaves.

marinade:

¾ CUP DRY WHITE WINE

2 TABLESPOONS OLIVE OIL

1 SMALL ONION, SLICED

3 OR 4 PIECES OF FRESH LEMON PEEL

1 TABLESPOON CHOPPED FRESH HERBS, SUCH AS PARSLEY, BASIL, OREGANO,
   TARRAGON, OR ROSEMARY, OR 1 TEASPOON DRIED HERBS

KOSHER SALT AND FRESHLY GROUND BLACK PEPPER

2 RED BELL PEPPERS, SEEDED, DEVEINED, AND QUARTERED

2 YELLOW OR ORANGE BELL PEPPERS, SEEDED, DEVEINED, AND QUARTERED

16 SCALLIONS, TRIMMED

12 EARS FRESH CORN, HUSKED

OLIVE OIL, FOR BRUSHING

KOSHER SALT AND FRESHLY GROUND BLACK PEPPER

1. In a medium bowl, combine the wine, olive oil, onion, lemon peel, herbs, and salt and pepper to taste. Put the peppers and scallions in a nonreactive bowl. Pour the marinade over them and toss well to coat. Marinate the vegetables for up to 30 minutes at room temperature or for 2 hours in the refrigerator.

2. Brush each ear of corn generously with olive oil and season with salt and pepper.

3. Prepare a gas or charcoal grill. Lay the corn on the grill rack and grill over medium-high heat for about 8 to 10 minutes, turning several times, until nicely browned. Lift the peppers and scallions out of the marinade and grill, turning once, about 4 minutes, until lightly charred and tender.

4. Remove from the grill, let the vegetables cool a bit and serve.

SERVES 6

seven hills *columbia valley, washington*

FEW WINERIES IN THE Northwest can boast residency in two different states, but Seven Hills Winery spent more than 10 years in Oregon before moving 10 miles down the road to its current location in Walla Walla, Washington.

Wine Enthusiast magazine lauds their "sensitive detailed winemaking." Seven Hills wines are known for their balance, a trinity of fruit, acidity, and tannins that makes the red wines delicious upon release as well as rewarding with cellar age. One of the stars is the Ciel du Cheval Vintage Red Wine, full of raspberry and plum flavors with hints of smoke and cedar. The focus of the winery is producing varietal red wine from Cabernet Sauvignon, Merlot, and Syrah grapes, all grown in the appellations of eastern Washington. Winemaker Casey McClellan also applies his deft touch to Pinot Gris, Riesling, and Viognier from northwest appellations.

black-bean salad

This salad is a wonderful accompaniment to grilled tuna. Be sure to allow time for soaking the beans. If you prepare this more than a few hours ahead of time, you may want to refresh the beans with a drizzle of olive oil just before serving.

3 CUPS DRIED BLACK BEANS

6 CUPS CHICKEN BROTH, PREFERABLY HOMEMADE

1 TABLESPOON DIJON MUSTARD

2 TABLESPOONS BALSAMIC VINEGAR

2 CLOVES GARLIC, FINELY MINCED

¾ CUP EXTRA-VIRGIN OLIVE OIL

KOSHER SALT AND FRESHLY GROUND BLACK PEPPER

4 SCALLIONS (WHITE AND GREEN PARTS) TRIMMED AND CUT INTO ½-INCH PIECES

1 MEDIUM RED ONION, THINLY SLICED

1. Pick over the beans, discarding any broken or misshapen ones and rinse thoroughly. Put the beans in a large pot or bowl, cover with about 2 inches of cold water, and soak for 6 to 8 hours or overnight.

2. Drain the beans and put them in a large soup pot. Add the chicken stock and bring to a boil over high heat. Reduce the heat, cover and simmer the beans for 45 to 60 minutes, until just tender. Be careful not to overcook.

3. Drain the beans and rinse them under cold, running water. Set aside in a large bowl to cool.

4. In a small bowl, combine the mustard, vinegar, and garlic. Slowly whisk in the olive oil until thick. Season the vinaigrette to taste with salt and pepper.

5. Add the scallions, red onion, and cilantro to the cooled beans. Toss gently. Pour the vinaigrette over the beans and toss well. Set aside for at least 1 hour to give the flavors time to blend. Or cover and refrigerate the salad for up to 12 hours before serving chilled or at room temperature.

SERVES 6

peach & raspberry cobbler

Peaches and raspberries speak of high summer when a simple fruit dessert is called for to end the meal.

1½ CUPS SIFTED UNBLEACHED ALL-PURPOSE FLOUR

¼ TEASPOON SALT

5 TABLESPOONS UNSALTED BUTTER, CHILLED

¼ CUP VEGETABLE SHORTENING, CHILLED

4 OR 5 TABLESPOONS ICE WATER

6 RIPE PEACHES, PEELED, PITTED AND THINLY SLICED (ABOUT 2½ POUNDS)

1 CUP FRESH RASPBERRIES

½ CUP SUGAR

3 TABLESPOONS UNSALTED BUTTER, CUT INTO PIECES

WHIPPED CREAM OR ICE CREAM, FOR GARNISH (OPTIONAL)

1. Preheat the oven to 450°F. Lightly butter a 7-by-9-inch baking dish.

2. Combine the flour, salt, butter and shortening in the bowl of a food processor and pulse until the mixture resembles coarse meal. Slowly add the ice water and process until the dough begins to hold together and gathers on the blade. Shape the dough into a ball, working in a little more flour if necessary. Wrap in waxed paper and refrigerate for 30 to 60 minutes.

continued

WINE PAIRING

•
Beaulieu Vineyard Muscat de Beaulieu
Benton-Lane Pinot Noir Rosé

••
Channing Daughters Mosaico
Cooper Mountain Vineyard Pinot Blanc 'Vin Glace'

•••
Chateau St. Jean Late Harvest Riesling 2005

3. Put the peaches and raspberries in a large bowl. Sprinkle the sugar over the fruit and toss together. Set aside at room temperature for about 15 minutes to give juices time to accumulate and sweeten.

4. On a lightly floured surface or on a piece of waxed paper and using a floured rolling pin, roll the dough into a rough 10-by-12-inch rectangle. Line the baking dish with the dough, allowing the excess to hang over the sides. Spoon the peach and raspberry mixture evenly over the dough and dot it with butter. Fold the overhanging dough back over the fruit. It will not cover the fruit but will form a decorative edge.

5. Put the cobbler on a center rack of the oven and immediately reduce the temperature to 425°F. Bake for 35 to 45 minutes, or until the crust is golden and the fruit is bubbling hot.

6. Spoon the cobbler, warm or at room temperature, into bowls. Serve with whipped cream or ice cream, if desired.

SERVES 6 TO 8

chateau st. jean   *sonoma valley, california*

CHATEAU ST. JEAN is notable for its exceptionally beautiful buildings, expansive landscaped grounds, and gourmet-market-like tasting room. The heart of the winery is a chateau built in the 1920s that is surrounded by formal estate gardens inspired by those in Italy and France. Among California wineries, Chateau St. Jean is a pioneer in vineyard designation—the process of making wine from, and naming it for, a single vineyard.

Winemaker Margo Van Staaveren is continuing the long tradition of crafting single-vineyard wines and currently makes a dozen, including the highly acclaimed Robert Young Vineyard Chardonnay, Belle Terre Chardonnay, and La Petite Étoile Fumé Blanc. To achieve the Chateau St. Jean single-vineyard designation, the grapes must consistently exhibit exceptional varietal character with each red, white, and dessert wine, showing the vineyard's unique *terroir*—"taste of the earth."

autumn menus

Take full advantage of farmers' markets and produce stands that are packed with gorgeous fruits and vegetables this time of year, and create a warm and wonderful autumn dinner.

slow-roasted cherry tomatoes

Here's a fabulous way to prepare cherry tomatoes. They make a great topping for grilled bread or crackers. You can also roast them whole and serve them on their own.

1½ POUNDS CHERRY TOMATOES, HALVED

2 GARLIC CLOVES, PEELED AND THINLY SLICED

3 TABLESPOONS EXTRA-VIRGIN OLIVE OIL

½ CUP BLACK OLIVES, PITTED AND HALVED

FRESHLY GROUND BLACK PEPPER

1. Preheat the oven to 325°F.

2. Put the tomatoes, garlic, and olive oil in a large roasting pan. Toss together and roast for 45 minutes. Remove from the oven and let cool to room temperature.

3. Add the olives and pepper to taste to the tomato mixture and gently stir.

4. Serve with grilled bread, mozzarella or ricotta cheese and chopped fresh herbs.

SERVES 6 TO 8

WINE PAIRING

•
Barboursville Pinot Grigio 2007

••
Lafond Vineyards Santa Rita Hills Pinot Noir

Rancho Sisquoc Pinot Noir 2006

•••
Goldeneye Anderson Valley Pinot Noir

Nickel & Nickel Spring Hill Vineyard Pinot Noir 2006

intimate autumn dinner

SLOW-ROASTED CHERRY TOMATOES

SPINACH & ARUGULA SALAD WITH WARM MUSHROOMS, OLIVES & PANCETTA

RISOTTO WITH BROCCOLI RABE & PARMESAN CHEESE

APPLE TART

rancho sisquoc   *santa maria valley, california*

RANCHO SISQUOC WINERY was one of the first wineries to open its doors in the now famous Santa Barbara County wine region, and is proud to have been creating award-winning wines for over 35 years. Located in northern Santa Barbara County, it is part of an historical Spanish land grant. The local Chumash Indians called the area *Sisquoc*, which meant "gathering place." Today the winery, which features a rustic, charming tasting room and beautiful picnic grounds, is indeed a gathering place for wine lovers. The winery crafts more than twelve varieties, all produced from grapes grown on the estate's 300-plus acres of vine-yards. The unique microclimates of the respective vineyards are responsible for the broad variation in flavor. A list of their standout wines would have to include Sylavner, Tre Vini, and Pinot Noir.

Rancho Sisquoc Winery is the only winery in California that produces Sylvaner, which is a Riesling blend. This favorite has hints of light lime, apricot, and sweet pear, with a crisp finish and a superb flavor. The Tre Vini is made from 50 percent Sangiovese, 27 percent Cabernet Sauvignon, and 23 percent Malbec. The Sangiovese gives this firm-bodied wine a lively cherry flavor, while the Malbec contributes some floral notes and chalky earth. The Cabernet gives it some fabulous black-jam flavors and it culminates in a jazzy finish headed by the Sangiovese. The Pinot Noir is a very approachable and easy-drinking wine with its juicy flavors, full palette, and smooth finish.

spinach & arugula salad
with warm mushrooms, olives & pancetta

This is a warm and wonderful salad to serve as a first course. The woodsy flavor of sautéed shiitake and cremini mushrooms adds a deep autumnal flavor to the spinach and arugula.

6 SLICES PANCETTA, ABOUT ⅛-INCH THICK, OR 4 SLICES THICK-CUT BACON

7 TABLESPOONS OLIVE OIL

½ POUND SHIITAKE MUSHROOMS, STEMMED AND THINLY SLICED

½ POUND DOMESTIC OR CREMINI MUSHROOMS, STEMMED AND THINLY SLICED

2 CLOVES GARLIC, THINLY SLICED

¼ CUP NIÇOISE OLIVES, PITTED AND HALVED

2 TABLESPOONS FRESH LEMON JUICE

1 TABLESPOON BALSAMIC VINEGAR

4 CUPS SPINACH OR BABY SPINACH, STEMMED, RINSED, AND PATTED DRY

2 CUPS TRIMMED ARUGULA, RINSED AND DRIED

FRESHLY GROUND BLACK PEPPER

1. In a skillet or sauté pan, fry the pancetta or bacon over medium heat until crisp. Drain on paper towels, cut into small pieces, and set aside.

2. Wipe out the pan with paper towels. Heat 3 tablespoons of the olive oil in the pan over medium-high heat. Add the mushrooms and sauté, stirring frequently, for 5 minutes. Reduce the heat to medium and stir in the garlic, olives, lemon juice, and vinegar. Simmer for 5 minutes to blend the flavors.

WINE PAIRING

●
Barboursville Vintage Rosé 2007

● ●
Beaulieu Vineyard Carneros Pinot Noir 2006
Clos Du Val Pinot Noir 2006
Peju Provence 2007
Rancho Sisquoc Sisquoc River Red 2006

● ● ●
Bedell Cellars Bedell Musée 2006
Goldeneye Anderson Valley Pinot Noir

3. Meanwhile, toss the spinach and arugula with the remaining 4 tablespoons olive oil in a large bowl. Season to taste with pepper. Add the warm mushroom mixture and the bacon to the greens and toss until well blended. Serve at once from the bowl or arrange on individual plates.

SERVES 6

risotto with broccoli rabe & parmesan cheese

Risotto tastes wonderful when it's prepared with assertive, pleasantly bitter broccoli rabe. This delectable Italian rice dish can be tricky to make, because while each grain of rice should be separate, the creamy sauce made from broth, butter, and cheese must bind the rice. To achieve the proper balance, be careful not to overcook the rice, and stir the risotto constantly during cooking.

6 TO 7 CUPS CHICKEN BROTH, PREFERABLY HOMEMADE

1 TABLESPOON UNSALTED BUTTER

2 TABLESPOONS EXTRA-VIRGIN OLIVE OIL

1/2 CUP FINELY CHOPPED SHALLOTS

3 CLOVES GARLIC, THINLY SLICED

2 CUPS ARBORIO RICE

1 BUNCH (1 TO 1 1/2 POUNDS) BROCCOLI RABE, TOUGH STEMS DISCARDED,
   AND CHOPPED INTO 1-INCH PIECES

1/2 CUP FINELY CHOPPED PARSLEY

3 TABLESPOONS FRESHLY GRATED PARMESAN CHEESE, PLUS MORE FOR SERVING

2 TABLESPOONS FRESH LEMON JUICE

KOSHER SALT AND FRESHLY GROUND BLACK PEPPER

1. In a large saucepan, bring the broth to a boil over high heat. Reduce the heat to maintain a simmer.

2. Meanwhile, heat the butter and oil in a large skillet over medium heat. Add the shallots and garlic and sauté for about 5 minutes, until soft. Add the rice and stir with a wooden spoon until the rice is well coated with butter and oil.

WINE PAIRING

•

Barboursville Chardonnay Reserve 2007

Chateau Ste. Michelle Columbia Valley
   Chardonnay 2006

••

Chateau St. Jean Sonoma County
   Pinot Noir 2006

Clos Du Val Merlot 2005

Seven Hills Ciel du Cheval Vineyard
   Vintage Red Wine Red Mountain 2006

•••

Merryvale Carneros Chardonnay 2006

Paraduxx Napa Valley Red Wine

3. Slowly add the simmering broth to the rice, a ladleful at a time. Stir constantly to prevent the rice from sticking. As soon as one ladleful of broth is absorbed by the rice, add the next. The entire process will take 15 to 20 minutes, and the rice should be tender but still firm.

4. Add the broccoli rabe, parsley, 3 tablespoons of Parmesan cheese, and lemon juice. Stir for about 5 minutes, tasting to test for doneness. The broccoli rabe will be crisp-tender. Season to taste with salt and pepper, and serve immediately with Parmesan cheese.

SERVES 6

PINOT NOIR

Pinot Noir grapes are produced in California, Oregon, Washington, and New York's Finger Lakes region. Because they are sensitive to temperature change and have delicate skins, these red grapes can be difficult to handle. Their flavors are reminiscent of sweet red berries, plums, and cherries, and they sometimes have a distinct earthy or woodsy flavor, depending on specific growing conditions.
Pinot Noir may be one of the world's most versatile food wines. It pairs well with poultry, beef, lamb, and pork. It is also an excellent wine to drink with pasta and rice dishes, cream sauces, and spicy foods.

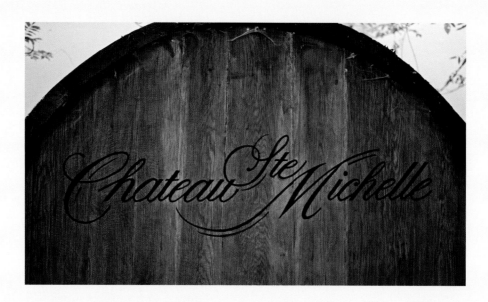

chateau ste. michelle *columbia valley, washington*

CHATEAU STE. MICHELLE is the oldest winery in Washington State, with some of the most mature vineyards in the Columbia Valley. The winery dates back to the period following the repeal of Prohibition and produces many highly acclaimed Chardonnays, Rieslings, Merlots, and Cabernets. Chateau Ste. Michelle has received some of the highest accolades in the industry, including American Winery of the Year 2004 from *Wine Enthusiast* magazine and 2005 Winery of the Year by *Restaurant Wine* magazine.

Chateau Ste. Michelle is the largest single producer of Riesling wine in the world, with up to seven different Rieslings that showcase the versatility of Riesling and regional styles within Washington's Columbia Valley. Their spectacular Columbia Valley Riesling exudes aromas of candied peach and pear, overripe apple, white cherry, and spice. Wine drinkers are in for a truly rare treat when the weather allows: Chateau Ste. Michelle's recent 2006 Eroica Riesling Ice Wine is an exotic, luscious, ultra-ripe wine with concentrated aromas and flavors of apricot and honey.

apple tart

This homey, autumnal dessert is always a hit and makes a wonderful ending for a sumptuous dinner. Northern Spy, Paula Red, and Winesaps are excellent varieties of apples to use for this pie.

crust:

6 TABLESPOONS (¾ STICK) UNSALTED BUTTER, CHILLED, CUT INTO SMALL PIECES

1 CUP UNBLEACHED ALL-PURPOSE FLOUR

2 TABLESPOONS SUGAR

2 TO 3 TABLESPOONS COLD WATER

filling:

3 APPLES, PEELED, HALVED, CORED, AND CUT INTO THIN SLICES

3 TABLESPOONS SUGAR

PINCH OF GROUND CINNAMON

3 TABLESPOONS UNSALTED BUTTER

2 TABLESPOONS CALVADOS

glaze:

3 TABLESPOONS APRICOT JAM

1 TABLESPOON WATER

WHIPPED CREAM OR VANILLA ICE CREAM (OPTIONAL), FOR SERVING

1. Prepare the crust: Put the butter, flour, and sugar in a food processor fitted with a steel blade and process just until the mixture resembles coarse meal. With the machine running, pour enough cold water through the feed tube to form a dough. Wrap in plastic wrap and refrigerate 30 minutes.

2. On a lightly floured surface, roll the dough into a 10½-inch circle. Line a 9-inch tart pan with a removable bottom with the dough; trim and crimp the edges decoratively. Put the tart pan in the freezer 15 to 20 minutes.

continued

3. Preheat the oven to 375°F.

4. Arrange the apple slices in a circle just inside the outer edge of the pan, slightly overlapping them. Fill in the interior ring, overlapping the remaining slices. Fill in any gaps with extra apple slices.

5. Mix the sugar and cinnamon together and sprinkle the mixture evenly over the apple slices. Dot with butter and drizzle with Calvados.

6. Bake the tart until light golden brown, about 45 minutes.

7. While the tart is baking, heat the apricot jam and the water in a small pan until the jam is melted. Brush the glaze evenly over the warm tart. Serve warm or at room temperature with whipped cream or ice cream, if desired.

SERVES 6 TO 8

WINE PAIRING

•
Rancho Sisquoc Sylvaner 2007

••
Barboursville Malvaxia Passito 2005
Benton-Lane Pinot Blanc

•••
Chateau Ste. Michelle Ethos Late
    Harvest Riesling 2006
Nickel & Nickel Sori Bricco
    Vineyard Merlot 2005
V. Sattui Mt. Veeder
    Cabernet Sauvignon 2005

CABERNET SAUVIGNON

A cross between Cabernet Franc and Sauvignon Blanc, Cabernet Sauvignon has the distinction of being the world's most sought after red wine. One of the most commonly planted grapes in California and Washington, it is gaining in popularity in the rest of the United States as well. Its high tannin content provides structure and intrigue while supporting a rich, ripe berry, tobacco, and sometimes green-pepper flavor. The aging potential can be upwards of 10 to 20 years, though 5 to 9 years is more usual. It pairs well with red meats, flavorful pastas, lamb, strong-flavored cheese, and dark chocolates.

barboursville *barboursville, virginia*

BARBOURSVILLE VINEYARDS was founded in 1976 by Gianni Zonin as the sole New World winery of the largest privately held enterprise in Italy. Dating from the 18th century and lying between Monticello and James Madison's Montpelier in the heart of the Virginia Piedmont, the estate is home to the landmark ruins of the residence Jefferson designed for his friend, Governor James Barbour.

Barboursville's renown in wine and food circles throughout the country rests on its status as the most-awarded winery in the region and for having brought to life the stunningly authentic and inventive Palladio Restaurant. Here, the hallmarks of regional vividness and varietal integrity in Barboursville wines, so widely admired in national competitions, are mirrored gastronomically by an invigoration of Northern Italian tradition with the choicest seasonal ingredients.

*Invigorating autumn days and busy schedules call for a time to slow down. Enjoy
a rich and satisfying Sunday dinner designed to take advantage of the season's bounty.*

wild mushroom soup

The liquid from dried wild mushrooms gives this soup a wonderfully
rich flavor. Although white button mushrooms may be used for fresh
mushrooms, cremini mushrooms have a stronger, more intense flavor.

2 OUNCES DRIED PORCINI MUSHROOMS

1 1/2 CUPS LUKEWARM WATER

2 TABLESPOONS UNSALTED BUTTER

1 TABLESPOON OLIVE OIL

3 LARGE LEEKS (WHITE AND GREEN PARTS), RINSED AND DICED
   (ABOUT 3 CUPS)

2 MEDIUM ONIONS, THINLY SLICED

1 POUND FRESH MUSHROOMS, PREFERABLY CREMINI,
   STEMMED AND THINLY SLICED

3 TABLESPOONS FLOUR

4 CUPS CHICKEN BROTH, PREFERABLY HOMEMADE

2 CUPS WATER

KOSHER SALT AND FRESHLY GROUND BLACK PEPPER

1/2 CUP MADEIRA WINE

1/2 CUP PLUS 3 TABLESPOONS CHOPPED FRESH PARSLEY

SOUR CREAM FOR GARNISH

1. Put the dried mushrooms in a bowl and add the lukewarm water. Soak for about 30 minutes. Lift out the mushrooms and set aside but do not discard the water. Strain the soaking water through a sieve lined with paper towels or a coffee filter and set aside.

2. In a stockpot, heat the butter and oil and over medium heat until the butter melts. Add the leeks and onions and cook for about 10 minutes, stirring often, until tender.

3. Set aside about ½ cup of the sliced fresh mushrooms to use for garnish. Add the remaining fresh mushrooms to the pot and cook for about 5 minutes until softened. Sprinkle with the flour and cook for an additional 5 minutes, stirring occasionally.

4. Add the chicken broth, water, soaked dried mushrooms, and the reserved strained soaking water. Add salt and several generous grindings of pepper. Bring to a boil, reduce the heat, and simmer uncovered for about 5 minutes, stirring occasionally, until the soup is heated through. Remove the soup from the heat and let it cool for about 10 minutes.

5. Purée the soup in batches in a food processor or blender until nearly smooth; the soup will retain some texture from the mushrooms. Return the soup to the pot and heat over low heat for about 5 minutes.

6. Stir in the wine and ½ cup of the parsley and cook, stirring occasionally, for about 5 minutes.

7. Ladle the soup into shallow bowls and top each serving with a dollop of sour cream, a few slices of mushrooms, and some chopped parsley.

SERVES 6

WINE PAIRING

•
Chateau Ste. Michelle Columbia Valley
    Chardonnay 2006

••
Beaulieu Vineyard Carneros
    Pinot Noir 2006

Bedell Cellars Bedell Estate Chardonnay
    2007

Gloria Ferrer Carneros Pinot Noir 2005

Peju Napa Valley Syrah 2005

•••
Goldeneye Anderson Valley
    Pinot Noir

Talley Vineyards Arroyo Grande Valley
    Estate Pinot Noir

bedell cellars *cutchogue, new york*

BEDELL CELLARS is built on the site of a 1919 potato barn which now serves as the tasting room. The facility is renowned for its sophistication and the contemporary art beautifully displayed in its distinctive surroundings.

Bedell's critically acclaimed blends, called Taste, Gallery, and Musée pair up with labels commissioned from artists Barbara Kruger, Ross Bleckner, and Chuck Close, respectively. *Wine Enthusiast* magazine declares, "The wines are classy but innovative and include white and red blends and the signature offering, Merlot." Now owned by Michael Lynne, former co-chairman and co-CEO of New Line Cinema, the winery caters to wine lovers year-round on the beautiful North Fork of Long Island.

pan-seared duck breasts with red-wine sauce

Here is a quick and elegant dish to serve for a special dinner party.

2 TABLESPOONS LIGHT SOY SAUCE

2 TABLESPOONS ORANGE JUICE

1 TEASPOON CHILI PASTE

2 TEASPOONS FIVE-SPICE POWDER

FRESHLY GROUND BLACK PEPPER

2 DUCK BREASTS, ABOUT 1 POUND EACH

2 TABLESPOONS UNSALTED BUTTER

2 SHALLOTS, MINCED

1 TEASPOON FRESH THYME LEAVES

1 CUP DRY RED WINE

¼ CUP GREEN OLIVES, PITTED AND HALVED

WINE PAIRING

•

Chateau Ste. Michelle Columbia Valley
Cabernet Sauvignon 2005

Sterling Vintner's Collection Shiraz

• •

Beaulieu Vineyard Coastal Estates Zinfandel
2005

Bedell Cellars Bedell Cabernet Franc 2006

Hedges Family Estate Three Vineyards 2006

Seven Hills Walla Walla Valley Malbec 2006

• • •

Duckhorn Vineyards Napa Valley Merlot

Gloria Ferrer Brut Rosé 2004

Lafond Chardonnay Lafond Vineyard

Merryvale Carneros Pinot Noir 2007

Peju Napa Valley Cabernet Franc 2005

1. In a small bowl, whisk together the soy sauce, orange juice, chili paste, five-spice powder, and pepper to taste. Score the fat side of the duck breasts in a criss-cross pattern. Pour the mixture over the duck. Cover and marinate in the refrigerator for 2 hours.

2. Preheat the oven to 250°F.

3. In a cast-iron skillet, sear the duck breasts over high heat until well browned on all sides. Transfer to a baking dish and bake for 45 minutes.

4. Melt 1 tablespoon of the butter in a skillet, add the shallots, and cook until softened. Stir in the thyme and half the wine. Cook until the wine reduces by one third. Remove from the heat.

5. A few minutes before serving, bring the sauce to a simmer. Stir in the remaining butter and wine, and simmer for 5 minutes, stirring occasionally. Add the olives and simmer for 5 more minutes.

continued

6. To serve, cut the duck on the bias into thin slices and arrange on a serving platter. Spoon the sauce over the duck and serve at once.

SERVES 6

wild rice

Nutty and aromatic wild rice goes very well with duck as well as many other poultry dishes. The general rule of thumb when cooking wild rice is three parts liquid to one part rice—however, different brands and styles of wild rice can vary, so it is best to read and follow package directions carefully.

1 CUP WILD RICE, RINSED AND DRAINED
2 CUPS WATER
1 CUP CHICKEN BROTH
1 TABLESPOON UNSALTED BUTTER OR OLIVE OIL
KOSHER SALT AND FRESHLY GROUND BLACK PEPPER
1/2 CUP CHOPPED FRESH FLAT-LEAF PARSLEY

1. Combine the wild rice, water, broth, and butter in a pan with a tight-fitting lid and bring to a boil. Reduce the heat, cover, and simmer 45 minutes. Do not remove the lid. Remove from the heat and let sit 10 minutes, or cook the wild rice according to package directions.
2. Before serving, fluff the rice with a fork. Season with salt and pepper to taste, garnish with the parsley and serve immediately.

SERVES 6

beaulieu   *napa valley, california*

BEAULIEU VINEYARD is one of Napa Valley's most historic wineries, founded in 1900 by Georges de Latour. A Napa Valley leader with more than 100 years of tradition in great wine-making, Beaulieu, French for "beautiful place," is dedicated to the creation of recognizable world-class wines that embody innovation and excellence. Beaulieu creates benchmark wines that define the heritage of Napa Valley.

Today, winemaker Joel Aiken continues the great tradition of finely crafted wines handed down to him by legendary Beaulieu winemaker Andre Tchelistcheff.

lemon green beans with toasted almonds

This knockout side dish makes delicious use of a few simple ingredients: fresh green beans, lemons, good olive oil, and lightly toasted almonds.

2 POUNDS FRESH GREEN BEANS, RINSED AND TRIMMED

JUICE OF 1/2 LEMON

2 TABLESPOONS EXTRA-VIRGIN OLIVE OIL

KOSHER SALT AND FRESHLY GROUND BLACK PEPPER

1/3 CUP LIGHTLY TOASTED CHOPPED ALMONDS

1. In a saucepan of boiling salted water, cook the beans for 4 to 5 minutes, until crisp-tender. Rinse under cold running water and drain. Transfer to a bowl and set aside.

2. In a small bowl, whisk together the lemon and oil and season to taste with salt and pepper. Pour over the beans and toss thoroughly. Sprinkle with the almonds and serve warm, chilled, or at room temperature.

SERVES 6

Toasting Nuts

To toast nuts, spread them on a baking sheet and toast them in a preheated oven or toaster oven for 3 to 5 minutes or until golden brown and fragrant. Shake the pan once or twice for even toasting. Slide them off the baking sheet as soon as they reach the desired color to halt the cooking. Let cool.

dolce   *napa valley, california*

DOLCE SWEET WINES are made through *botrytis cinerea*, or "noble rot," which yields some of the greatest sweet late-harvest wines of the world, with ultra-concentrated sugars, aromas, and flavors. Napa Valley's Dolce Winery is the only winery in North America that is solely devoted to producing a single late-harvest wine.

Dolce is made with grapes grown on a 27-acre vineyard in the Coombsville region east of the town of Napa. The Semillon and Sauvignon Blanc vines are planted in well-drained volcanic soils near the Vaca Mountains. The first vintage of Dolce was made in 1985, but it was not released commercially until 1992 (1989 vintage).

As *botrytis cinerea* forms inconsistently from year to year, production has varied from a few hundred to a few thousand cases. Picking grapes with *botrytis cinerea* is very labor-intensive, as several passes are required to pick each berry at the optimum time. Dolce's most recent release is the 2005 vintage.

vanilla-scented poached pears

Here is a simple and elegant recipe for poached pears. It's best to make them a day ahead of time, which is great for dinner-party advance planning—great-tasting, too.

WINE PAIRING

•

Bedell Cellars Bedell First Crush White 2007

• •

Benton-Lane Pinot Blanc

Cooper Mountain Vineyard Pinot Blanc 'Vin Glace'

Mumm Napa Brut Prestige

• • •

Dolce 2005

6 BOSC PEARS, PEELED, WITH STEMS INTACT

1/2 CUP SUGAR

4 CUPS FRUITY RED WINE

1/3 CUP CRÈME DE CASSIS

2 TABLESPOONS FRESH LEMON JUICE

1 VANILLA BEAN, SPLIT LENGTHWISE

6 WHOLE CLOVES

2 CINNAMON STICKS

WHIPPED CREAM, FOR SERVING (OPTIONAL)

1. Trim the bottoms of the pears so that they can sit upright. Put them in a large nonreactive saucepan.

2. Mix the sugar, wine, crème de cassis, and lemon juice together and pour over the pears. Add the vanilla bean, cloves, and cinnamon sticks.

3. Cover the pan and bring the liquid to a simmer over medium heat. Simmer, partially covered, for about 30 minutes, turning the pears occasionally, until they are cooked through and evenly colored.

4. Remove the pan from the heat and let the pears cool in the liquid. Transfer both the pears and liquid to a glass or ceramic bowl. Cover and refrigerate for 24 hours before serving. Serve chilled or at room temperature with whipped cream, if desired.

SERVES 6

far niente

napa valley, california

THIS STONE WINERY, straight out of a storybook, has a tale to match. Founded by John Benson in 1885, Far Niente prospered until the onset of Prohibition in 1919, when the winery ceased operation and the buildings and estate were abandoned. Sixty years later, in 1979, Gil and Beth Nickel purchased the old stone shell of a winery and spent three years restoring the building to its original 19th-century grandeur. During restoration, the name *Far Niente*, which, romantically translated means "without a care," was found carved in stone on the front of the building.

In 1998, Far Niente was reunited with its past when a bottle of 1886 Far Niente Sweet Muscat was found in a wine cellar in Marin County, California, fully intact with its original cork, capsule, and label.

Now on the National Register of Historic Places, Far Niente produces critically acclaimed Chardonnay and Cabernet Sauvignon renowned for their consistent house style and ability to evolve with extended age.

Spend a delightful afternoon or evening with family and friends hosting a wine-and-cheese party.
This casually elegant style of gathering is just right for any occasion.

wine & cheese party

ASSORTED CHEESES:
HARD CHEESE,
SEMI-FIRM CHEESE,
BLUE CHEESE,
SEMI-SOFT CHEESE,
SOFT-RIPENED CHEESE,
DOUBLE & TRIPLE CRÈME
CHEESE,
CHÈVRES

ASSORTED
FRESH & DRIED FRUITS

HONEY, FIG JAM,
CHERRY PRESERVES

ASSORTED NUTS

wine & cheese party

The choice of wines to serve with cheese is wide and varied—from light and simple whites to rich, dense reds—and the fun part of this stylish get-together is sipping and tasting a variety of wines and cheeses and discovering new tastes and pairings.

For exceptional color and taste, add a selection of fresh fruits, such as apples, pears, plums, figs, and grapes, and dried fruits, such as apricots and raisins, to the cheese platter. Condiments such as wild honey, fig jam and cherry preserves, and walnuts, almonds, and pistachios also are wonderful accompaniments.

When selecting cheese for a party, think in terms of taste, texture, and contrast, and be sure to serve cheese at room temperature—never cold. Cut just before serving to avoid drying out.

There are different categories of cheese, and it's a nice idea to choose a few cheeses from each one. The following pages offer a sampling.

Hard Cheeses

Hard cheeses are often only thought of as "grating cheese." But many hard cheeses are packed with flavor and deserve a place on any great cheese plate.

Asiago: This cheese is made from part-skim cow's milk. It has a rich, nutty flavor and is good with peasant bread and black olives.

Dry Jack: This is a Monterey Jack cheese that is aged 6 months to 2 years. It is reminiscent of Parmesan but is less grainy. It is very good with apples and plums.

Parmigiano-Reggiano: The king of Italian cheeses has a wonderful, rich, nutty flavor and is well worth its price. Although it is best known as the cheese to be grated over pasta, it is also a superb dessert cheese. It is especially good with ripe pears and walnuts.

WINE PAIRING

●●●

Clos du Val Stags Leap District
    Cabernet Sauvignon 2004

Duckhorn Vineyards Napa Valley Merlot

Far Niente Estate Bottled
    Cabernet Sauvignon

Semi-Firm Cheeses

The range of cheeses in this category is wide—from aged sheep's milk to Cheddar to Swiss-style cheeses. They're all quite wonderful and should be well-represented on the cheese platter.

Aged Sheep's-Milk Cheese: There is a variety of these delicious cheeses from all over the world to choose from. Among them are Prince de Claverolle and Etorki, from France's Western Pyrénées; Brin d'Amour, from Corsica; Pecorino Toscano, the sheep's-milk cheeses made in Tuscany, and Manchego, from the Castilla-La Mancha region in Spain. These cheeses have a piquant and nutty flavor.

Cheddar: There are a good number of Cheddars to choose from. Among them are Black Diamond Cheddar, from Canada; Grafton Village and Shelbourne Farms, from Vermont, and Tillamook Cheddar, from Oregon. Cheddar cheese is delicious with apples and grapes.

Emmenthaler: The original golden Swiss cheese has a distinctly nutty flavor. It is very good with apples, cherries, and plums.

Gruyère: This heartier, nuttier Swiss is best known for its use in fondues, quiches, and tarts. But is also very good when served on its own or with thinly sliced sausage or salami. Comté, a french Gruyère, is a bit firmer and drier, and goes well with a mild sausage.

WINE PAIRING

●●

Zaca Mesa Black Bear Syrah 2004

●●●

Far Niente Estate Bottled Chardonnay

Goldeneye Anderson Valley Pinot Noir

Paraduxx Napa Valley Red Wine

Blue Cheeses

Blue cheeses range from soft, creamy, and mild to intense and firm. They pair beautifully with a variety of wines. Here are a few examples of excellent blue cheeses.

Blue de Bresse: A creamy, mild blue cheese from France. It is lovely to serve with fresh figs.

Gorgonzola: This rich and pungent cheese from Italy is a very good addition to a dessert cheese plate alongside ripe apples, pears, and walnuts.

Maytag Blue: This tangy blue from Maytag Dairy Farms in Iowa is delicious served with poached pears.

Roquefort: This pungent, aged sheep's-milk blue cheese is from France. It has a soft, creamy texture and goes well with figs and nuts.

Stilton: This assertive blue-mold cheese is from England. It has a very rich flavor and aftertaste. It is excellent with grapes.

Semi-Soft Cheeses

The smooth and buttery flavors and soft textures of these semi-soft cheeses make them perennial party favorites to serve with a variety of wines.

Fontina: This creamy cow's-milk cheese has a mild, nutty flavor. Although it is best known as an Italian cheese, Fontina is also made in Denmark, France, and the U.S.

Edam & Gouda: These good, all-purpose cheeses from Holland go well with apples and pears.

Morbier: This aromatic cow's-milk cheese from France is defined by the dark vein of vegetable ash that streaks through its center. It has a subtle, nutty taste.

WINE PAIRING

••
Barboursville Nebbiolo Reserve 2005

•••
Duckhorn Vineyards Napa Valley
   Cabernet Sauvignon

Far Niente Estate Bottled
   Cabernet Sauvignon

Peju Napa Valley Cabernet Franc 2005

Muenster: The flavor of French muenster cheese ranges from mild to assertive, depending on its aging time. This style of muenster cheese bears no resemblance to American supermarket muenster cheeses.

Port Salut: This cow's-milk cheese has a mild, creamy flavor and a very smooth texture. It is excellent with olives.

Reblechon: When perfectly ripe, this French cow's-milk cheese has a mild and delicate flavor and should be eaten then. Because it continues to ripen after refrigeration, it can become bitter when overripe.

Taleggio: The flavor of this rich cheese from the Lombardy region of Italy can range from mild to pungent as it ages. It is very good with fresh peaches, plums, and cherries.

WINE PAIRING

•

Chateau Ste. Michelle Columbia Valley
　　Riesling 2007

••

Channing Daughters Rosso Fresco

Cooper Mountain Vineyard Pinot Gris
　　'Old Vines'

•••

Zaca Mesa Roussanne 2006

Soft-Ripened Cheeses

These cheeses are big crowd-pleasers and good choices for parties. Look for cheese with a clean white rind—if the rind has lines, dark spots, or a brownish tinge, the cheese may be overripe and no longer desirable. Try to buy a whole wheel of cheese rather than a wedge cut from a larger wheel.

Brie: Brie is probably the most popular French cheese in this country. It has a smooth and buttery flavor. To check for ripeness, the cheese should be supple, not stiff to the touch. Brie is delicious when served with crisp baguettes and juicy ripe peaches, pears, and grapes.

Camembert: This is a wonderful rich and creamy cheese. Good, buttery Camemberts include the popular Valée and Le Chatelaine brands from France and the superb Blythedale Farms from Vermont. Be careful not to cut Camembert before it is fully ripened or it will never achieve its full potential.

WINE PAIRING

••

Channing Daughters Vino Bianco

Chateau Ste. Michelle Canoe Ridge Estate
　　Chardonnay 2006

Cooper Mountain Vineyard Pinot Noir
　　Reserve

Peju Provence 2007

Double and Triple Crème Cheeses

These rich and luscious cow's-milk cheeses are enriched with cream. Double crème cheeses contain a minimum of 60 percent butterfat and triple crèmes must have at least 75 percent. These soft and subtly sweet cheeses are delicate, so it is best to buy them whole instead of in cuts.

L'Explorateur: This delicious triple crème has a delightfully smooth flavor and a rich, buttery texture.

Saint André: This creamy, buttery triple crème has a mildly sweet finish.

WINE PAIRING

•
Chateau Ste. Michelle Domaine
    Ste. Michelle Blanc de Blancs
••
Channing Daughters Rosato di Merlot
Peju Napa Valley Chardonnay 2007

Chèvres

Goat cheese, also known as *chèvre,* has a distinctive tart and tangy flavor. Although some of the better-known chèvres, such as Boucheron and Montrachet, are produced in France, there are many wonderful farmstead goat cheeses being produced domestically. These tangy goat's-milk cheeses are very good with olives, capers, and fruity olive oil. They are also delicious served with figs, berries, and grapes for dessert.

Boucheron: These well-known, log-shaped chèvres have a buttery texture and medium-tart flavor.

Crottin: These button-shaped goat cheeses are lovely to serve drizzled with olive oil and fresh herbs.

Montrachet: This well-known white chèvre from Burgundy has a soft, creamy texture. It is excellent with figs and nuts.

Fresh chèvres: Although these luscious fresh cheeses used to be rare in this country, small farms from regions all over the country are producing excellent handcrafted cheeses. A few good ones to look for are Laura Chenel, from California; Coach Farms, from New York, and Consider Bardwell, from Vermont.

WINE PAIRING

•
Barboursville Vintage Rosé 2007
••
Chateau Ste. Michelle Horse Heaven
    Sauvignon Blanc 2006
Cooper Mountain Vineyard Pinot Gris
    Reserve
•••
Channing Daughters Mudd Vineyard
    Sauvignon Blanc
Far Niente Estate Bottled Cabernet
    Sauvignon
Peju Napa Valley Sauvignon Blanc 2007

winter menus

Left: Sanford Winery & Vineyards, Santa Rita Hills, California

A casual and cozy brunch is a great way to get together with friends during the winter months. Mimosas made with sparkling wine, or a glass of Chardonnay or Merlot, add a festive touch.

swiss chard frittata

Swiss chard is a versatile green with a delicious, earthy flavor and, like most greens, is easy to find during the colder months. It is especially good in a simple frittata. It's just the thing for a breakfast or brunch party, as it is easy to assemble and bakes in less than 30 minutes. And because frittata can be served at room temperature, it can wait until your guests are at the table.

1 LARGE BUNCH (ABOUT 1½ POUNDS) GREEN OR RED
  SWISS CHARD, STEMMED

1 TABLESPOON UNSALTED BUTTER

1 TABLESPOON EXTRA-VIRGIN OLIVE OIL

1 TABLESPOON MINCED SHALLOTS

2 TABLESPOONS MINCED ONION

5 LARGE EGGS

¼ CUP HALF-AND-HALF

¼ TEASPOON NUTMEG

SALT AND FRESHLY GROUND BLACK PEPPER

½ CUP FRESHLY GRATED GRUYÈRE CHEESE

3 TABLESPOONS FRESHLY GRATED PARMESAN CHEESE

continued

cozy brunch

SWISS CHARD FRITTATA

ROASTED POTATOES
& CARAMELIZED SHALLOTS

MIXED GREENS
WITH HERBED VINAIGRETTE

GRILLED PEASANT BREAD

CAFÉ AU LAIT

ORANGE & POMEGRANATE
JUICE MIMOSAS

WINE PAIRING

•

Barboursville Chardonnay 2006

Chateau St. Jean Sonoma County
    Chardonnay 2006

• •

Benton-Lane Pinot Gris 2007

Cooper Mountain Vineyard Pinot Gris Reserve

Seven Hills Pinot Gris 2007

• • •

Duckhorn Napa Valley Merlot

Far Niente Estate Bottled Chardonnay 2006

1. Preheat the oven to 350°F.

2. Put the chard in a vegetable steamer over boiling water, cover, and cook over medium heat for 5 to 8 minutes until tender. Drain well, chop coarsely, and set aside.

3. Heat the butter and oil in a large skillet over medium-high heat until foaming. When foam begins to subside, add the shallots and onion and cook for 2 to 3 minutes, just until translucent. Stir in the chopped chard, mix well, and remove from the heat.

4. Butter a 10-inch round glass or ceramic baking dish or an 11¾-by-7½-inch rectangular glass baking dish. Spread the Swiss chard mixture evenly in the dish.

5. In a bowl, combine the eggs, half-and-half, and nutmeg, and season to taste with salt and pepper. Whisk well to combine, add the Gruyère cheese and whisk again. Pour the egg mixture over the chard and sprinkle with the Parmesan cheese. Bake for 25 to 30 minutes, until the top is lightly browned.

6. Let cool slightly and serve warm, or serve at room temperature.

SERVES 6

duckhorn   *napa valley, california*

CO-FOUNDED BY Dan and Margaret Duckhorn in 1976, Duckhorn Vineyards have been crafting classic Bordeaux varietals from the Napa Valley for nearly 30 years. This winemaking tradition has grown to include seven meticulously farmed estate vineyards located throughout the various microclimates of the Napa Valley. Focused on quality and consistency, these estate vineyards are an essential element in making wines of distinction. One of the first wineries to pioneer Merlot as a premium varietal, Duckhorn Vineyards now makes several elegant Merlot and distinctive Cabernet Sauvignon bottlings to showcase the characteristics of its various vineyard sites. In addition, the winery produces a full-flavored Sauvignon Blanc and an exceptional red Bordeaux blend under the Decoy label.

roasted potatoes & caramelized shallots

A savory mix of slow-cooked potatoes and shallots is an ideal dish for brunch. Gentle oven roasting allows them to caramelize and develop a full, rounded flavor. It's easy: simply toss the potatoes, shallots and herbs with fruity olive oil, and roast.

16 UNPEELED SMALL RED NEW POTATOES (ABOUT 3 POUNDS),
    HALVED OR QUARTERED

16 SHALLOTS, PEELED

3 TABLESPOONS EXTRA-VIRGIN OLIVE OIL, PLUS MORE FOR SERVING (OPTIONAL)

1 TEASPOON CHOPPED FRESH THYME LEAVES

1 TEASPOON CHOPPED FRESH ROSEMARY LEAVES

KOSHER SALT AND FRESHLY GROUND BLACK PEPPER

1. Preheat the oven to 300°F.

2. In a roasting pan, toss the potatoes and shallots together with the olive oil, thyme, rosemary, and salt and pepper to taste. Roast, tossing 2 or 3 times, 1½ to 2 hours, until the vegetables are fork-tender.

3. Arrange the vegetables in a shallow bowl or a large platter. Drizzle with a bit of additional olive oil, if desired. Serve warm.

SERVES 6

cooper mountain   *cooper mountain, oregon*

NESTLED ON THE SIDE of an ancient volcano, the Cooper Mountain Vineyards focuses exclusively on growing organic grapes. Specializing in Pinot Noir, Pinot Gris, and Chardonnay, Cooper Mountain got its start in 1978 when Dr. Robert Gross and his wife, Corrine, planted the first Pinot Noir and Chardonnay vines on the site. Expanding from there, the winery opened in 1987 and achieved its organic status in 1995.

The winery currently produces five varietals as well as a balsamic vinegar, Apicio, made in a classical Italian style.

benton-lane *willamette valley, oregon*

BENTON-LANE WINERY, which produces wines exclusively from their Certified Sustainable estate vineyard, is one of only a few 100 percent family-owned Oregon wineries. Founded in 1988 by Steve and Carol Girard, Benton-Lane creates silky, flavorful Pinot Noir from their 138-acre vineyard near Monroe, Oregon, in the Willamette Valley.

As part of their goal to minimize soil inputs, their vineyards are not only Certified Sustainable but also Certified Salmon Safe. Benton-Lane is also the first winery in Oregon to maximize wine quality to the consumer by eliminating all cork closures.

The winery recently won the "Top 100 Wines of the World" award for Pinot Noir from *Wine Spectator* magazine and the same award from *Wine & Spirits* magazine for Pinot Gris.

mixed greens
with herbed vinaigrette

This salad is sublime in its simplicity and is a beautiful accompaniment to the frittata and potatoes.
Serve with warm, crusty peasant bread.

vinaigrette:

¼ CUP CHAMPAGNE VINEGAR

¾ CUP GRAPESEED OIL

1 TABLESPOON MINCED FRESH THYME

2 FRESH BASIL LEAVES, MINCED

SALT AND FRESHLY GROUND BLACK PEPPER

4 CUPS MIXED SALAD GREENS

1. In a small bowl, whisk together the vinegar, oil, thyme, basil,
and salt and pepper to taste. Cover and refrigerate for 1 hour.
2. Toss the salad with enough vinaigrette to coat the greens
and serve.

SERVES 6

café au lait

A cup of warm café au lait is the perfect way to get started on a weekend morning. It's a nice idea to serve it with with a choice of condiments so your guests can customize their coffee.

4 CUPS OF WHOLE MILK

4½ CUPS OF FRESHLY BREWED COFFEE OR ESPRESSO

coffee condiments:

SUGAR

HONEY

COCOA POWDER

GROUND CINNAMON

In a medium saucepan, heat the milk until bubbles begin to form around the edge of the pan. Whisk the milk until it begins to thicken. Transfer to an insulated pitcher or coffee carafe. Slowly add the coffee to the milk and stir gently to combine. Serve at once in large mugs or bowls with the condiments.

SERVES 6

SPARKLING WINES

Because they offer great bargains and are every bit as festive, sparkling wines are a wonderful alternative to Champagne. Many of these wines are made using the traditional *methode champenoise* technique, which involves taking various still wines and blending them before putting them through a secondary fermentation in the bottle, which produces the bubbles. Sparkling wines from California and Oregon feature Chardonnay, Pinot Noir, and Pinot Meunier grapes and are very close in style to French Champagne. They pair well with smoked salmon, shellfish, and pork and duck dishes. They also make excellent aperitifs, and mix well with fresh fruit juices for those perennial brunch favorites, mimosas and Bellinis.

orange & pomegranate juice mimosas

Traditional mimosas are made with Champagne or sparkling wine and orange juice. A mix of orange and pomegranate juice is a wonderful alternative and lovely to serve for a weekend brunch party.

4 CUPS ORANGE JUICE

⅓ CUP POMEGRANATE JUICE

ONE 750-ML BOTTLE CHAMPAGNE OR SPARKLING WINE, CHILLED

Mix the orange juice and pomegranate juice together in a large pitcher. Fill flutes or goblets halfway with the juice mixture and add the Champagne or sparkling wine. Serve at once.

MAKES 12 MIMOSAS

nickel & nickel *napa valley, california*

ESTABLISHED IN 1997 by the partners of Far Niente, Nickel & Nickel is devoted exclusively to producing 100 percent varietal, single-vineyard wines that best express the distinctive personality of each vineyard. The winery is based in Oakville, California, on the 42-acre John C. Sullenger vineyard property, named after a prospector who struck gold in the Sierra Nevada and was the first to develop the site. The winery completed construction of a cutting-edge facility housed within a vintage 1880s farmstead in the summer of 2003, when it officially opened to the public.

Winemaker and president Darice Spinelli says, "Our goal is not to interfere with the vineyards to make the wines taste the way we want them to. Rather, we consider it our job to accentuate the vineyard and play up the special characteristics of each site, whether we're dealing with ten rows or ten acres."

Come in from the cold and enjoy an intimate comfort-food supper in front of the fire. Lamb stew paired with full-bodied red wine will warm your soul.

winter comfort-food supper

BLUE CHEESE CAESAR SALAD

OVEN-BRAISED LAMB & WHITE-BEAN STEW

BREAD PUDDING WITH RED PLUMS

blue cheese caesar salad

Classic Caesar salad is composed of romaine lettuce, Parmesan cheese and dressing made from oil, fresh lemon juice, Worcestershire sauce and a raw egg. Most people also think that this classic salad includes anchovies. This version includes homemade croutons and omits the raw egg altogether. It's topped with blue cheese, and the anchovies are optional.

- 3/4 CUP EXTRA-VIRGIN OLIVE OIL
- 4 LARGE CLOVES GARLIC, PEELED
- 4 CUPS 1/2-INCH CUBES FRENCH OR ITALIAN BREAD (ABOUT HALF A BAGUETTE)
- KOSHER SALT
- 1 LARGE OR 2 MEDIUM HEADS ROMAINE LETTUCE, DRAINED AND PATTED DRY
- JUICE OF 1 LEMON
- 1/4 CUP WORCESTERSHIRE SAUCE
- 1/2 CUP (2 OUNCES) FRESHLY GRATED PARMESAN CHEESE
- FRESHLY GROUND BLACK PEPPER
- 6 OUNCES BLUE CHEESE, CRUMBLED
- 8 ANCHOVY FILETS, DRAINED (OPTIONAL)

1. The day before making the salad, mix the olive oil and garlic together in a jar, cover, and set aside. For more intense garlic flavor, cut one of the cloves in half.

2. In a large skillet, heat ¼ cup of the garlic-flavored oil over medium heat. Add the bread cubes, sprinkle with a little salt, and sauté for about 15 minutes, shaking and turning to coat the bread until golden. Lift the croutons from the pan with a slotted spoon and set aside to drain on paper towels.

3. Tear the romaine lettuce leaves into good-sized pieces and put them in a large salad bowl. Add 6 tablespoons of the oil and toss to coat the leaves thoroughly. Add the lemon juice and Worcestershire sauce and toss again. Season to taste with salt.

4. Add the Parmesan cheese and remaining 2 tablespoons oil and toss. Toss in the croutons and season to taste with pepper.

5. Arrange the salad on chilled dinner plates and top with blue cheese. Add anchovies, if desired. Serve immediately.

SERVES 6

WINE PAIRING

•

Beaulieu Vineyard Coastal Estates
  Chardonnay 2006

••

Chateau Ste. Michelle Indian Wells
  Merlot 2005

Clos Du Val Chardonnay 2006

•••

Artesa Limited Release Merlot 2003

Merryvale Napa Valley Merlot 2005

Nickel & Nickel John's Creek Vineyard
  Chardonnay 2006

oven-braised lamb & white-bean stew

This one-dish wonder is welcome winter fare and it's especially good to serve for an intimate dinner because its flavor improves and intensifies if made a day or two ahead of time.

beans:

1 POUND DRIED WHITE BEANS, SUCH AS CANNELLINI OR GREAT NORTHERN

4 CUPS WATER

2 CUPS CHICKEN BROTH

1 ONION, PEELED AND HALVED

1 CARROT, PEELED AND HALVED CROSSWISE

6 SPRIGS FRESH THYME

KOSHER SALT AND FRESHLY GROUND BLACK PEPPER

stew:

2½ POUNDS LAMB STEW MEAT, CUT INTO 2-INCH CUBES

KOSHER SALT AND FRESHLY GROUND BLACK PEPPER

3 TABLESPOONS OLIVE OIL

1 ONION, PEELED AND CHOPPED

1 CARROT, PEELED AND CHOPPED

4 CLOVES GARLIC, THINLY SLICED

1½ CUPS DRY WHITE WINE

1 CUP FRESH OR CANNED PLUM TOMATOES, COARSELY CHOPPED, WITH JUICE

1 CUP CHICKEN BROTH

KOSHER SALT AND FRESHLY GROUND BLACK PEPPER

½ CUP CHOPPED FRESH PARSLEY, FOR GARNISH

continued

1. To prepare the beans, rinse them and put them in a large saucepan. Cover with cold water. Cover the pan and bring the water to a boil over high heat. Remove the pan from the heat. Let rest, covered, for 40 minutes.

2. Drain the beans, discarding the cooking liquid. Add the 4 cups of water, the chicken broth, onion, carrot, thyme, and salt and pepper to taste. Bring to a simmer over medium heat and cook, uncovered, until the beans are tender, about 45 minutes. The beans should be firm-tender. Drain beans and discard the onion, carrot, and thyme. (The beans may be cooked in advance and then reheated.)

3. To prepare the stew, pat the lamb dry and sprinkle with salt and pepper. Heat 2 tablespoons of the oil over medium-high heat in a large soup pot or Dutch oven. When the oil is hot but not smoking, add the lamb in batches and brown on all sides, 5 to 7 minutes for each batch. Transfer the lamb with a slotted spoon to a bowl and wipe out the pot.

4. Heat the remaining 1 tablespoon of olive oil in the pot, add the onion and cook over medium heat until it begins to brown, about 5 minutes. Add the carrot and garlic and cook until softened, about 3 minutes.

5. Pour in the wine and bring to a boil, scraping up any brown bits from the pan. Add the tomatoes and their juice, chicken broth, and salt and pepper to taste. Return the lamb and its juices to the pot. Bring to a boil, reduce the heat to low, and simmer, covered, for 30 minutes.

6. Preheat the oven to 325°F.

7. Add the beans to the lamb and a bit of water or wine if the mixture seems dry. (The stew may be prepared up to this point and will keep in the refrigerator for up to 2 days. Bring to room temperature before final cooking.) Bring to a simmer, cover, and transfer to the oven. Bake for 45 minutes. Uncover and bake 30 to 45 minutes, until most of the liquid is absorbed.

8. To serve, divide the stew into soup bowls, garnish with parsley, and serve at once.

SERVES 6

WINE PAIRING

•

Sterling Vintner's Collection Shiraz 2005

••

Chateau St. Jean Sonoma County Merlot 2005

Cuvaison Napa Valley Carneros Syrah 2006

Gloria Ferrer Carneros Syrah 2004

Hedges Family Estate Three Vineyards 2006

•••

Clos Du Val Stags Leap District Cabernet Sauvignon 2004

Duckhorn Vineyards Napa Valley Cabernet Sauvignon

Talley Vineyards Stone Corral Vineyard Pinot Noir

Willamette Valley Vineyards Tualatin Estate Vineyard Pinot Noir 2006

bread pudding with red plums

Bread pudding is a satisfying dessert to make on a chilly evening, and it is very good with a spoonful of vanilla ice cream or whipped cream.

1 TABLESPOON UNSALTED BUTTER

7 CUPS FRENCH OR ITALIAN BREAD PIECES,
    TORN INTO 1-INCH CHUNKS

3 CUPS MILK

4 EGGS

1/2 CUP PLUS 2 TABLESPOONS SUGAR

4 LARGE RED PLUMS, PITTED AND CUT INTO 1/4-INCH SLICES
    (ABOUT 1 1/2 CUPS)

1/4 TEASPOON GROUND CINNAMON

1 TEASPOON FRESH LEMON JUICE

VANILLA ICE CREAM OR WHIPPED CREAM
    FOR SERVING (OPTIONAL)

1. Preheat the oven to 350°F. Butter a 2-quart glass or ceramic baking dish.

2. Put the bread in a large bowl, pour the milk over it, and let sit for about 15 minutes so that the bread absorbs the milk.

3. Beat the eggs with 1/2 cup of the sugar until smooth. Pour the egg mixture into the soaked bread and mix gently. Scrape this mixture into the baking dish.

4. Arrange the plum slices in even rows over the top of the pudding. Mix together the cinnamon and the remaining 2 tablespoons sugar and sprinkle over the plums. Sprinkle the lemon juice over the plums.

5. Bake for 35 to 40 minutes, until the pudding is just lightly browned. Let cool slightly. Serve with ice cream or whipped cream, if desired.

SERVES 6

WINE PAIRING

•
Benton-Lane Pinot Noir Rosé
Chateau Ste. Michelle
    Columbia Valley Syrah 2003
••
V. Sattui Family Red 2006
Zaca Mesa Late Harvest Viognier 2006
•••
Dolce 2005

zaca mesa   *santa ynez valley, california*

LOCATED IN THE NORTHERNMOST portion of Santa Ynez Valley, Zaca Mesa is only 30 miles from the Pacific Ocean. Unlike most parts of the California coast, its valleys are oriented east-west, thus opening directly to the cooling marine influences that include morning fog and afternoon breezes, making the vineyard a uniquely perfect site for growing grapes.

During the late 1970s, the Zaca Mesa Winery pioneered Syrah plantings in the warm eastern parts of the Santa Ynez Valley. The wines have been consistently impressive since 1993. Made from the first Syrah grapes planted in Santa Barbara County, the Syrah wines are rich in blackberry, cassis, mocha, cedar, and signature sage spice aromas and flavors.

After attempting to grow a wide variety of grapes, Zaca Mesa focused its efforts on the grape varieties of the Rhône Valley of France because they thrive in the microclimate of its heavenly valley. Their decision was rewarded when the Syrah became the first, and so far only, Santa Barbara wine named in the Top 10 gracing *Wine Spectator's* Top 100 wine list.

Ring in the holidays with an open-house buffet. Whether for lunch, cocktail hour, or dinner, a buffet can be prepared well ahead of time and set out at the last minute, with delicious results.

warm mixed olives

Here is an excellent way to prepare olives: Marinate them with an orange, fresh herbs, and spices, and sauté them in a bit olive oil just before serving. These warm, aromatic olives have a rich, meaty flavor.

1 POUND ASSORTED OLIVES,
   SUCH AS KALAMATA, GAETA, AND PICHOLINE
1 SMALL ORANGE CUT INTO 6 WEDGES
1 TABLESPOON CHOPPED FRESH ROSEMARY
1 TEASPOON FENNEL SEEDS
1 TEASPOON CORIANDER SEEDS
PINCH OF RED PEPPER FLAKES
2 TABLESPOONS OLIVE OIL
2 CLOVES GARLIC, THINLY SLICED

1. Drain the olives if in brine. Combine the olives, orange, rosemary, fennel seeds, coriander seeds, and red pepper flakes, and mix well. Cover and refrigerate, stirring occasionally.

2. Heat the oil in a skillet and sauté the garlic over medium heat until softened, about 2 minutes. Add the olive mixture and simmer, stirring occasionally, until heated through, about 10 minutes. Remove the orange pieces and serve warm.

MAKES ABOUT 3 CUPS

holiday open house

WARM MIXED OLIVES

SPICY PECANS

ROASTED EGGPLANT DIP
WITH HANDMADE PITA CRISPS

FOCACCIA SQUARES
WITH CARAMELIZED ONIONS
& GOAT CHEESE

GINGER-SOY CHICKEN WINGS

SHRIMP WITH GARLIC-CHILI
MAYONNAISE

SMOKED TROUT SPREAD

PROSCIUTTO-WRAPPED FIGS

ASSORTED PATÉS & MEATS,
CHEESES, BREADS & CRACKERS

spicy pecans

There is a pleasant kick to these spice and cocoa-coated nuts. They can be made up to a week ahead of time and stored in airtight containers. These tasty nuts will disappear from the buffet table fast.

VEGETABLE OIL TO GREASE THE BAKING SHEETS

1 EGG WHITE

4 CUPS (ABOUT 1 POUND) PECAN HALVES

1/3 CUP SUGAR

1 TABLESPOON UNSWEETENED COCOA POWDER

2 TEASPOONS CHILI POWDER

1 TEASPOON GROUND CUMIN

1/2 TEASPOON GROUND GINGER

1/4 TEASPOON GROUND CLOVES

KOSHER SALT AND FRESHLY GROUND BLACK PEPPER

1. Preheat the oven to 350°F. Lightly oil two baking sheets.

2. In a large bowl, beat egg white until frothy. Add the pecans and toss well to coat.

3. In a small bowl, combine the sugar, cocoa powder, chili powder, cumin, ginger, and cloves. Add to the pecans and toss well to coat evenly. Divide the nuts evenly between the baking sheets, and spread in a single layer. Sprinkle generously with salt and pepper to taste. Bake for 15 minutes, shaking the pan occasionally.

4. Remove the baking sheets from the oven. Sprinkle with more salt and pepper, if desired. Let rest for 2 hours. The nuts will keep for up to a week stored in airtight containers.

MAKES 4 CUPS

WINE PAIRING

•
Barboursville Pinot Grigio 2007

• •
Seven Hills Walla Walla Valley Syrah 2005
Willamette Valley Vineyards Willamette Valley Pinot Noir 2006
Zaca Mesa Roussanne 2007

• • •
Paraduxx Napa Valley Red Wine

willamette valley   *willamette valley, oregon*

FOUNDED IN 1983 by Jim Bernau, Willamette Valley Vineyards specializes in growing,
by hand, the highest quality Pinot Noir, Pinot Gris, and Chardonnay grapes. Each wine is
truly expressive of the varietal as well as the place where the grapes are grown. With stylistic
emphasis on pure varietal fruit characters, Willamette Valley gives special attention to depth,
richness of "mouth," feel, and balance. This devotion to quality in the vineyard and winery is
only equaled by Jim Bernau's longstanding commitment to environmental stewardship. Bernau
believes that wines made with consideration for the environment, employees, and community
simply taste better.

Carved into the top of an ancient volcanic flow overlooking the hills of Salem, Oregon,
the winery, with its underground cellar, offers spectacular sweeping views of the Willamette
Valley below.

roasted eggplant dip

This full-flavored dip is excellent with handmade pita crisps.

2 SMALL EGGPLANTS

4 GARLIC CLOVES, THINLY SLICED

KOSHER SALT AND FRESHLY GROUND BLACK PEPPER

2 TABLESPOONS EXTRA-VIRGIN OLIVE OIL

2 TABLESPOONS FRESH LEMON JUICE

1 1/2 TEASPOONS GROUND CUMIN

PINCH OF RED PEPPER FLAKES

2 TABLESPOONS CHOPPED FRESH BASIL

2 TABLESPOONS CHOPPED FRESH FLAT-LEAF PARSLEY

1. Preheat the oven to 350°F.

2. Cut the eggplants in half lengthwise and make several deep slits in the flesh. Insert the garlic slices into the cuts. Put the eggplants on a baking sheet, sprinkle with salt and pepper to taste, and bake until tender, about 1 hour.

3. Remove the eggplants and drain on paper towels, cut side down. When cool enough to handle, scrape the eggplant flesh into a mixing bowl and mash with a fork. Stir in the olive oil, lemon juice, cumin, red pepper flakes, basil, and parsley. Taste and adjust the seasonings. The dip will keep, covered in the refrigerator, for up to 2 days.

MAKES ABOUT 2 CUPS

WINE PAIRING

•

Peju Napa Valley Syrah 2005

Rancho Sisquoc Cabernet Sauvignon 2005

Seven Hills Walla Walla Valley Syrah 2005

••

Benton-Lane Pinot Gris 2007

Cuvaison Napa Valley Carneros Merlot 2005

•••

Goldeneye Anderson Valley Pinot Noir

handmade pita crisps

These pita crisps are terrific accompaniments to roasted eggplant dip as well all kinds of other dips, spreads, and salsas.

¾ CUP OLIVE OIL

2 TEASPOONS PAPRIKA

TEN 6-INCH PITA POCKETS

KOSHER SALT

1. Preheat the oven to 350°F.

2. In a small bowl, stir together the olive oil and paprika.

3. Using a sharp knife, halve the pitas horizontally. Brush the rough sides of the pitas with the paprika oil and season generously with salt.

4. Cut each pita half into 7 or 8 wedges and arrange them in single layers on large, ungreased baking sheets. Bake in the middle of the oven for about 10 minutes, or until lightly browned and crisp. Cool on wire racks before serving. The pita crisps can be made up to 2 days ahead of time and stored in resealable plastic bags at room temperature.

MAKES ABOUT 12 DOZEN CRISPS

SYRAH or SHIRAZ

Syrah (known as Shiraz in Australia and South Africa) grapes produce medium- to full-bodied red wines that tend to be characterized by peppery and blackberry flavors. The most full-bodied Syrah wines also have notes of leather, roasted nuts, and spice. With their lush flavor, Syrah wines pair well with rich meat dishes and grilled vegetables.

cuvaison
estate wines
napa valley, california

EVERYTHING AT CUVAISON'S, from growing the grapes to making the wine, is about creating balance and length. Founded in 1969, Cuvaison's Mount Veeder and Carneros Estates produce Cabernet Sauvignon, Petite Verdot, Malbec, Cabernet Franc, and Zinfandel characterized as intense and black-fruited with powerful tannins. All of these grapes thrive in Cuvaison's Napa Valley microclimate, the heart of the Mt. Veeder Estate being the historic 170-acre Brandlin Vineyard located on the southwest side of the Valley.

Winemaker Steven Rogstad sums it up best: "My style and philosophy are based on expressing the unique character of our estate grapes and doing as little as possible to them. When one has such wonderful fruit to work with, that should be one's emphasis."

In 2007, the winery converted to solar power and is a Certified Sustainable and green business.

focaccia squares
with caramelized onions & goat cheese

Easy-to-make focaccia topped with goat cheese makes a simply elegant appetizer. It's also great with crumbled blue cheese.

focaccia:

2 CUPS ALL-PURPOSE UNBLEACHED WHITE FLOUR

2 TEASPOONS BAKING POWDER

3/4 TEASPOON SALT

3/4 CUP WHOLE MILK

1/4 CUP OLIVE OIL

2 TABLESPOONS (1/4 STICK) UNSALTED BUTTER, MELTED

topping:

2 TABLESPOONS (1/4 STICK) UNSALTED BUTTER

2 TABLESPOONS OLIVE OIL

2 LARGE RED ONIONS (ABOUT 1 1/2 POUNDS), HALVED AND THINLY SLICED

1 TEASPOON SUGAR

1 TABLESPOON CHOPPED FRESH ROSEMARY

KOSHER SALT AND FRESHLY GROUND BLACK PEPPER

1 CUP CRUMBLED GOAT CHEESE

1. To make the focaccia: Preheat the oven to 425°F. In a medium bowl, mix the flour, baking powder, and salt together. Make a well in the center of the dry ingredients. Whisk the milk, olive oil, and melted butter together in a liquid measuring cup. Slowly pour the milk mixture into the well and stir until just blended and smooth. Roll out the dough on a lightly floured surface to a 10-by-13-inch rectangle.

2. Transfer the the dough to a rimmed baking sheet and pierce all over with a fork. Let the dough rest while preparing topping.

3. To make the topping, melt the butter with oil in a large skillet over medium-high heat. Add the onions and cook until soft and beginning to brown, stirring frequently, about 10 minutes. Add the sugar, rosemary, and salt and pepper to taste. Reduce the heat to low and continue to cook until onions are soft and dark brown, stirring frequently, about 20 minutes. Set aside to cool.

4. Spread the onion mixture evenly over the dough. Sprinkle with the cheese. Bake until the crust is golden and the cheese is bubbly, about 20 minutes. Let cool. Cut into squares and serve.

MAKES ABOUT 42 SQUARES

WINE PAIRING

•
Sterling Napa County Sauvignon Blanc 2007
• •
Chateau St. Jean Sonoma County
   Cabernet Sauvignon 2005
Cooper Mountain Vineyard Pinot Gris
Fox Run Vineyards Cabernet Franc
• • •
Goldeneye Anderson Valley Pinot Noir 2005
Merryvale Carneros Chardonnay 2006
Peju Napa Valley Fifty/Fifty Red Wine 2005

CABERNET FRANC

Produced in Washington, California, New York's Finger Lakes region, and Long Island, Cabernet Franc is usually mixed with Cabernet Sauvignon or Merlot and sometimes both. Its fruity flavor, reminiscent of blueberry, raspberry, and plum, makes it a great accompaniment to spiced cuisine, such as food from the Middle East, as well as poultry, vegetable, and cheese dishes.

lafond   *santa rita hills, california*

FOUNDED BY PIERRE LAFOND in 1998, Lafond Winery & Vineyard has expanded from its initial 65 acres to just under 100 acres today. Lafond is a sister winery to Santa Barbara Winery, the first post-Prohibition winery in Santa Barbara County. Located in Santa Ynez Valley, Lafond is in the heart of Pinot Noir country, with soil and microclimates exceedingly favorable to that fickle grape variety. The climate, moderated by the Mojave Desert to the east and the Pacific Ocean to the west, is ideal for full-bodied grapes. The main plantings are Pinot Noir, Chardonnay, and Syrah, with smaller sections of Riesling and Grenache.

ginger-soy chicken wings

These tasty wings are a great party dish because they can be marinated a day ahead of time and quickly broiled just before serving.

3 TABLESPOONS SOY SAUCE

2 TABLESPOONS DRY SAKE

1 TABLESPOON HONEY

2 SCALLIONS, TRIMMED AND MINCED

1 TABLESPOON FINELY MINCED GARLIC

1 TABLESPOON FINELY MINCED GINGER

1 SMALL CHILE, TRIMMED AND FINELY MINCED,
   OR ¼ TEASPOON RED PEPPER FLAKES

3 POUNDS CHICKEN WINGS, WINGTIPS REMOVED, DRUMETTES AND WINGS SEPARATED

2 TABLESPOONS TOASTED SESAME SEEDS

1. In a small bowl, mix the soy sauce, sake, honey, scallions, garlic, ginger, and chile together. Put the chicken wings in a large nonreactive baking dish and pour the marinade over them. Cover and refrigerate for at least 2 hours or overnight. Turn the wings occasionally in the marinade.

2. Preheat the broiler. Remove the wings from the marinade and arrange them in 1 layer in a baking dish or broiler pan lined with aluminum foil. The pan should be 6 to 8 inches from the heat. Cook for about 10 minutes on each side, remove from the heat. Sprinkle the wings with sesame seeds and serve within 30 minutes.

SERVES 6

WINE PAIRING

•

Barboursville Pinot Grigio 2007

••

Cooper Mountain Vineyard Pinot Noir

Lafond Santa Rita Hills Chardonnay

Gloria Ferrer Napa Valley Carneros
   Chardonnay 2006

Rancho Sisquoc Tre Vini 2005

•••

Artesa Limited Release Chardonnay 2006

Merryvale Carneros Pinot Noir 2007

shrimp with garlic-chili mayonnaise

Shrimp is always a big hit at a cocktail party or buffet. Here it is served with a spicy homemade mayonnaise that can be made ahead of time.

shrimp:

2 CLOVES GARLIC, PEELED

KOSHER SALT

2 POUNDS MEDIUM SHRIMP, PEELED AND DEVEINED

garlic-chili mayonnaise:

3 LARGE CLOVES GARLIC, PEELED AND HALVED

PINCH OF RED PEPPER FLAKES

1 EGG, AT ROOM TEMPERATURE

1 EGG YOLK, AT ROOM TEMPERATURE

PINCH OF SALT

1 TABLESPOON FRESH LEMON JUICE

1/2 CUP CORN OIL

1/2 CUP OLIVE OIL

WINE PAIRING

•

Barboursville Chardonnay Reserve 2007

••

Bedell Cellars Bedell Taste White 2007

Channing Daughters Blaufruänkisch

Mumm Napa Brut Prestige

•••

Far Niente Napa Valley
    Estate Bottled Chardonnay 2006

1. To prepare the shrimp: Bring a large pot of water to a boil. Drop the garlic in the water and season with salt. When it boils, add the shrimp and cook for about 3 minutes, until just cooked through. Drain the shrimp and run under cool water. Cover and refrigerate for up to 6 hours before serving.

2. To prepare the mayonnaise: In a blender or food processor, pulse the garlic and red pepper flakes until minced. Add the egg, egg yolk, salt, and lemon juice, and pulse until fluffy, about 30 seconds. With the machine running, add the oils in a very slow, thin stream until all of the oil is incorporated. Taste and adjust the seasonings, if necessary. Cover and refrigerate for up to 6 hours before serving.

SERVES 12; MAKES ABOUT 1 CUP MAYONNAISE

smoked trout spread

Smooth, smoky trout spread served on triangles of toasted pumpernickel and topped with slices of cucumber and dill is delicious and refreshing.

3/4 CUP WHOLE MILK RICOTTA CHEESE

3/4 CUP LOW-FAT SOUR CREAM

1 POUND SMOKED TROUT FILET, CUT INTO SMALL PIECES (SEE NOTE)

2 TABLESPOON PREPARED HORSERADISH, DRAINED

4 SCALLIONS, TRIMMED AND MINCED

2 TABLESPOONS CHOPPED FRESH DILL

1 TEASPOON FRESH LEMON JUICE

FRESHLY GROUND BLACK PEPPER

24 SMALL SLICES OF PUMPERNICKEL BREAD,
   TOASTED AND CUT INTO TRIANGLES

2 CUCUMBERS, PEELED AND THINLY SLICED

DILL SPRIGS, FOR GARNISH

WINE PAIRING

•

Chateau Ste. Michelle Columbia Valley
   Syrah 2003

••

Barboursville [unoaked] Viognier
   Reserve 2006

Chateau St. Jean La Petite Étoile
   Fumé Blanc 2006

•••

Artesa Alexander Valley Cabernet
   Sauvignon 2004

Seven Hills Walla Walla Valley
   Pentad Vintage Red Wine 2005

Talley Vineyards Rincon Vineyard
   Pinot Noir

1. Place the ricotta cheese, sour cream, smoked trout, horseradish, scallions, dill, lemon juice, and pepper to taste in a food processor. Process until smooth. Taste and adjust the seasonings and process again. Scrape into a bowl, cover, and chill in the refrigerator 2 to 3 hours before serving.

2. Spread the pumpernickel toasts with the trout mixture and top with cucumber slices. Garnish each toast with a dill sprig and serve.

Note: Smoked trout is available in fish markets and specialty markets where high quality smoked fish is sold.

MAKES ABOUT 48 TOASTS

merryvale *napa valley, california*

MERRYVALE VINEYARDS is a family-owned Napa Valley Winery dedicated to passionate winemaking and the fine art of living well. For the past 25 years, Merryvale has been turning exceptional Napa Valley grapes into world-class wines, including powerful Cabernet Sauvignon and elegant Chardonnay. Merryvale's historic building was the first winery built in the Napa Valley after the repeal of Prohibition in 1933, and has become a must-see attraction for visitors to the valley.

Merryvale is committed to protecting and preserving the environment through sustainable farming practices. The recently built Starmont Winery on the historic Stanly Ranch in Carneros is a state-of-the-art solar-powered facility, and the estate vineyard at Starmont has received Napa Green Farm certification.

prosciutto-wrapped figs

This lovely appetizer is a delicious addition to a holiday buffet table. The flavor combination of sweet, ripe figs and salty prosciutto is unbeatable.

12 PAPER-THIN SLICES OF PROSCIUTTO, CUT INTO STRIPS

4 OUNCES PARMESAN CHEESE SHAVINGS

6 RIPE FIGS, QUARTERED

FRESHLY GROUND BLACK PEPPER

EXTRA-VIRGIN OLIVE OIL, FOR DRIZZLING (OPTIONAL)

WINE PAIRING

•
Benton-Lane Pinot Noir Rosé
Rancho Sisquoc Sauvignon Blanc 2007

• •
Clos Du Val Merlot 2005
Zaca Mesa Z Cuvée 2005

• • •
Bedell Cellars Bedell Musée 2006
Goldeneye Anderson Valley Pinot Noir
Merryvale Carneros Chardonnay 2006
Nickel & Nickel C.C. Ranch
    Cabernet Sauvignon 2005

Lay out a few strips of prosciutto. Put a few Parmesan shavings over them. Put a fig quarter on top and sprinkle with fresh black pepper. Roll up and arrange, seam side down, on a serving platter. Secure with a toothpick, if desired. Repeat with the remaining prosciutto, Parmesan, figs, and pepper. Just before serving, drizzle lightly with olive oil, if desired, and sprinkle with extra grated Parmesan.

Note: If you can't find fresh figs you may substitute dried figs or melon. You can also use softened blue cheese instead of Parmesan.

SERVES 12

index

TABLE OF EQUIVALENTS

The exact equivalents in the following tables have been rounded for convenience.

LIQUID/DRY MEASURES

U.S.	Metric
¼ teaspoon	1.25 milliliters
½ teaspoon	2.5 milliliters
1 teaspoon	5 milliliters
1 tablespoon (3 teaspoons)	15 milliliters
1 fluid ounce (2 tablespoons)	30 milliliters
¼ cup	60 milliliters
⅓ cup	80 milliliters
½ cup	120 milliliters
1 cup	240 milliliters
1 pint (2 cups)	480 milliliters
1 quart (4 cups, 32 ounces)	960 milliliters
1 gallon (4 quarts)	3.84 liters
1 ounce (by weight)	28 grams
1 pound	454 grams
2.2 pounds	1 kilogram

OVEN TEMPERATURES

Fahrenheit	Celsius	Gas
250	120	½
275	140	1
300	150	2
325	160	3
350	180	4
375	190	5
400	200	6
425	220	7
450	230	8
475	240	9
500	260	10

LENGTHS

U.S.	Metric
⅛ inch	3 millimeters
¼ inch	6 millimeters
½ inch	12 millimeters
1 inch	2.5 centimeters

Published in 2009 by Welcome Books®
An imprint of Welcome Enterprises, Inc.
6 West 18th Street, New York, NY 10011
Tel: 212-989-3200; Fax: 212-989-3205
www.welcomebooks.com

Publisher: Lena Tabori
Project Director: Alice Wong
Project Assistant: Robyn Curtis
Art Director and Designer: Barbara Scott-Goodman
Food and Prop Stylist: Paul Lowe
Winery consultants: Eric Nelson Norgaard, Earl Norgard, and Lori Olson

Library of Congress Cataloging-in-Publication Data

Scott-Goodman, Barbara.
  The vineyard cookbook seasonal recipes and wine pairings inspired by America's vineyards / by Barbara Scott-Goodman; food photography
by Colin Cooke ; with landscape photography by Kirk Irwin and Wes Walker.
      p. cm.
  Includes index.
  ISBN 978-1-59962-064-0
  1. Cookery (Wine) I. Title.
  TX726.S43 2009
  641.6'22--dc22

                                        2008045788

Printed in China
First Edition
10 9 8 7 6 5 4 3 2